THE NATURE OF LAW

BY

Thomas E. Davitt, S.J., Ph.D.

School of Law
St. Louis University

B. HERDER BOOK CO.
15 & 17 SOUTH BROADWAY, ST. LOUIS 2, MO.
AND
33 QUEEN SQUARE, LONDON, W. C.
1953

Library of Congress Catalog Card Number: 51-7687

Vail-Ballou Press, Inc., Binghamton and New York

It belongs to the reason
to direct to the end,
which is the first principle
in matters of action.

> St. Thomas, *Summa theol.*, Ia IIae,
> q. 90, a. 1, c.

CONTENTS

INTRODUCTION

This book is a historical introduction to a problem. The problem is the nature of law, that is, the relation between the concept of law and the philosophy of intellect and will.

It is an introduction, first, because it does not pretend to consider all the authors who may have contributed to the development of this problem and, secondly, because it does not profess to treat everything that the authors who are considered may have said on the subject.

What the work does propose to do, however, is primarily to consider those texts of certain authors which convey their main thought on this subject,[1] and secondarily to indicate which of the two solutions that will be encountered seems preferable and the reason why. As occasion offers, related questions that still need further investigation will also be pointed out.

The problem that concerns us here has its roots deep in the history of the philosophy of intellect and will. Without a knowledge of this history the problem itself cannot be fully understood, and unless it is, it will be approached with a cast of mind that precludes seeing the direction in

[1] Because of the fact that, for those interested, the original Latin texts are available, it has been considered unnecessary to reprint them here. Exact references will be given for every statement attributed to an author; statements are either close paraphrases or translations. (All translations, from whatever language, are the present author's and will be indicated by quotation marks.)

which the solution lies.[2] There is, therefore, a necessity for examining the period in which this philosophy grew and matured. This period, in general, extends from the thirteenth to the early seventeenth century. The philosophizing about law before this period (for instance, of Plato, Aristotle, Cicero, Gaius, Ulpian) was more of a general nature, lacking as it did a well worked out philosophy of man's intellect and will that could serve as a means of refining the concept of law. The thinking about law that followed this period even until today (as found, for instance, in Grotius, Hobbes, Pufendorf, Savigny, Wolff, Kant, Bentham, Holmes, and many others) either drew directly upon the riches amassed during this period or gradually fell away from the heights then attained according as the philosophy of man's nature was lost sight of. The sociological notion of law so prevalent today, based as it is on no definite philosophy of man, is a prime example of this. It is to authors, therefore, of the vital middle period that we must give our attention.

Since the thirteenth century two philosophies of intellect and will have developed: the one based on the primacy of the will, the other founded upon the primacy of the intellect.

The proponents of the primacy of the will vindicate the will's freedom of election by a complete causal independence of the will from the intellect. The cause of the freedom of election is solely in the will. The function of the intellect is only that of a *conditio sine qua non*. The dear-

2 Cf. below, p. 226, notes 3 and 4.

est aim of this group is to keep the will autonomous, to keep it completely independent of any physical necessity that might be imposed upon it by the intellect. Man is essentially a free creature.

Those who hold the primacy of the intellect, on the other hand, explain the freedom of election by a causal dependence of the will upon the intellect. Freedom of election has its metaphysical source in the intellect. The interaction of the intellect and will is one of mutual causality. Man is essentially a knowing creature.

In other words, the question is: What is the nature of the will? Is the will, in the act of choice, of such a nature that the action of the intellect with it is only that of a prerequisite condition? Or is the nature of the will such that it depends causally upon the intellect in the very act of choice? To express the problem in its metaphysical implications: Is the will the principle not only of *motus* but also of *ordo,* or is the will the source of motion, while the intellect alone is the principle of order?

These are radical divergencies and their results on the practical level are enormous. If the will is conceived as autonomous, then it alone can direct and command; and since command is law, law becomes an act of the will. Further, because the will can be put under no physical necessity by the intellect, neither can it be subjected to moral necessity by the intellect presenting means as necessary for an end. Hence the source of moral necessity, of obligation, is subjective—the will itself! In this system of thought, order and finality are to be found within the will.

On the other hand, if the will is conceived as having its metaphysical root in the intellect, then, of course, direction and command can pertain only to the intellect. Hence law is an act of the intellect. And since the intellect is allowed a causal interaction with the will, it can impose upon the will the moral necessity of acting according to the relation of means to an end that it might propose. The source of obligation is, then, for this group the objective relation of means necessary to attain an end.[3] Here objective order and finality, attained by the intellect, are outside the will.[4]

In the first of these positions where obligation depends upon the will of the lawgiver, a law that would not oblige directly in regard to the thing commanded but only to the payment of the penalty if the lawgiver so willed, is quite conceivable; and civil life is, in large part, not directly a matter of conscience. In the second position where obligation does not depend upon the will of the lawgiver but upon the objective nature of means necessary to attain an end, a law that would not oblige directly in regard to the thing commanded is wholly illogical and unthinkable; and every act of civil life has immediately some moral connotation, great or small. Of importance also is the fact that the relation between the concept of law and its foundation in psychology is basically the same as that of con-

---

[3] This necessity, of course, includes means that are both absolutely and relatively necessary to attain an end. Even such a contingent thing as, for instance, a traffic law is somehow necessary for the attainment of the common good.

[4] The importance of finality in determining the nature of the intellect and will is also shown in the specification of the moral act. See the excellent work of J. Rohmer, *La finalité morale chez les théologiens de Saint Augustin à Duns Scot* (Paris: Vrin, 1939).

tract, vow, and prayer.[5] Such then are, in general, the two positions we are about to examine.

Francis Suarez, S.J., writing in the seventeenth century and summarizing the opinions of those who had written before him, clearly indicates the relation of the concept of law to the philosophy of intellect and will. For, he says, those men have held that law is an act of the will who held that command is an act of the will. As witnesses to this he calls upon Henry of Ghent, John Duns Scotus, O.F.M., William Ockham, O.F.M., Gabriel Biel, and Alphonse de Castro, O.F.M.[6] Since these men played so important a part in the development of this position and especially in the formation of the mind of Suarez, one of its final great exponents, they, together with Suarez, will constitute one group to which we shall give our attention.

On the other hand, St. Thomas, writing in the thirteenth century, also points out the relation of the concept of law to the philosophy of intellect and will, and his thought crystallized in favor of law being an act of the intellect, and obligation being founded upon the objective relation of means to end. To law, he says, it pertains to command. Command, however, being an act of the intellect, law is also an act of the intellect.[7] Since St. Thomas was influenced by his master, St. Albert, and because certain authors who embraced and expounded St. Thomas were of such importance later, the other group to which we shall turn our attention will be composed of St. Albert, O.P., St. Thomas himself, Thomas de Vio (Cajetan),

[5] Cf. below, chap. 6, note 39.
[6] Suarez, *De legibus*, I, c.5, n.6.
[7] *Summa theologiae*, I–II, q.90, a.1, *sed contra*.

O.P., Dominic Soto, O.P., Bartholomew Medina, O.P., and St. Robert Bellarmine, S.J.[8]

Our method will be to examine first the philosophy of intellect and will of each author inasmuch as it has a relation to law and obligation. In this regard, a knowledge of the prudential series [9] in general is presupposed, and only those aspects of it will be treated in individual authors which have a bearing on our problem. Secondly, the author's position on law and obligation will be examined, as well as the relation he makes explicitly or implicitly between it and his psychology. Likewise here, a knowledge of the general theory of law [10] is presupposed, and only that part of an author's treatment will be given which directly contributes to our purpose.

Though various kinds of law may be considered throughout our inquiry, it is well to remember that what is said of them as law is true of all law.

[8] The reason why certain other authors have been omitted from these two groups will be indicated below: cf. pp. 24, 148, 161.

[9] Cf. Lottin, *Principes de morale* (Louvain: Mt. César, 1947), I, 252–66; the excellent article, "Prudence," by Noble, *Dictionnaire de théologie catholique*, XIII, 1023–76; M. Cronin, *The Science of Ethics* (Dublin: Gill and Son, 1939), I, 593–632.

[10] For the general idea of law, see A.–D. Sertillanges, O.P., *La philosophie des lois* (Paris: Alsatia, 1946); Molien, "Lois," *Dictionnaire de théologie catholique*, IX (1926), 871–910; M. Cronin, *op. cit.*, pp. 633–59.

Part One

THE PRIMACY OF THE WILL IN THE CONCEPT OF LAW

CHAPTER I

HENRY OF GHENT

I

HENRY OF GHENT (1217?–93) stands at the head of a long line of eminent men who held the primacy of the will both in their psychology and in their philosophy of law and obligation. The question may well be asked: What was it that disposed these men to consider the will rather than the intellect the superior faculty?

As far as Henry of Ghent is concerned, a partial answer to this question may be found by considering the conditions under which he lived. Henry was a master in theology at the University of Paris from 1276 until 1292. Averroism, with its doctrine of the unity of the agent intellect, the eternity of the world, and especially the negation of free choice, had first been condemned in 1270. In 1277 a second condemnation followed, and among the condemned propositions were some that were aimed at St. Thomas' teaching, especially his doctrine on free choice.

As Henry viewed Thomism he saw in it only a dangerous invasion of theology by pagan and infidel philosophy. Being genuinely disquieted, then, and thoroughly suspicious of Averroism and Thomism, he took an active part in bringing about their condemnation and served as ad-

visor to Etienne Tempier, the bishop of Paris, who promulgated both condemnations.[1]

As a consequence, Henry's whole doctrinal approach
was at a different angle from that of St. Thomas. Matter
could exist without form; there was no real distinction between *esse* and *essentia;* the principle of individuation was
not matter but a negation of divisibility; the human intellect depended on divine illumination in the act of cognition; and—what concerns us most here—the will, and not
the intellect, was the prime faculty. This last point is the
clue to the principal historical antecedents of Henry,
namely, the teachings of Augustine.

Augustine had given great emphasis to charity, saying
that charity is the one thing commanded by the Scrip-
tures [2] and that it is nothing else but a good will.[3] Proceeding further, Augustine tended to rule out external
purpose and finality in the action of the will. The reason
for the will's action, he said, was to be found *within* the
will itself.[4] Such an emphasis on the will—as the faculty
in which charity, the greatest of virtues, resides and the
power which finds the cause for its action within itself—
could not help but result in a doctrine of the primacy of
the will.[5]

---

[1] For a fuller account of these condemnations, see Etienne Gilson, *La philosophie au moyen âge* (Paris: Payot, 1947), pp. 558 f. Concerning Henry's works
and influence, see *ibid.*, pp. 427 f., and M. de Wulf, *Etudes sur Henri de Gand*
(Paris, 1897).

[2] St. Augustine, *De doctrina Christiana*, n. 15 (Migne, *PL*, XXXIV, 71).

[3] *Enarrationes in Psalmos*, 36, serm. 2, n. 13 (*PL*, XXXVI, 371). Cf. also *De
Trinitate*, Lib. VIII, cap. 10, n. 14 (*PL*, XLII, 960); *Epistolae 167 ad Hierony-
mum*, cap. 4, n. 15 (*PL*, XXXIII, 739).

[4] *De diversis quaestionibus*, LXXXIII, Lib. I, cap. 30 (*PL*, XL, 20); cf. *Enarrationes in Psalmos*, 55, n. 17 (*PL*, XXXVI, 658).

[5] As Professor Gilson says, ". . . the will in this doctrine necessarily becomes

It should be noted, too, that Anselm, upon whom Henry also draws, made Augustine's primacy of the will the foundation for his theory of justification.[6] In fact, it became the very definition of justice itself. For Anselm, justice is the rectitude of the will preserved *solely on account of itself*,[7] and for no other end outside the will.[8] As a consequence, the will in electing can be under no necessity.[9] In fact, liberty itself is defined in terms of this power of preserving rectitude for no other reason than on account of rectitude itself. This is *liberum arbitrium* and free will.[10]

Will pre-eminent. What are the reasons given by Henry for deciding that the will is superior to the intellect? Henry

---

the dominant faculty of the human soul" (*Introduction à l'étude de S. Augustin* [Paris: Vrin, 1931], p. 295).

[6] For Anselm's dependence on Augustine, see C. Filliatre, *La philosophie de Saint Anselme, ses principes, sa nature, son influence* (Paris: Alcan, 1920), p. 17.

[7] *De veritate*, cap. 12 (*PL*, CLVIII, 482); cf. *De concord. praesc. Dei cum lib. arbit.*, cap. 6 (*PL*, CLVIII, 516).

[8] *Ibid.* (483).

[9] *De concordia praescientiae Dei cum libero arbitrio*, cap. 6 (*PL*, CLVIII, 516). The question may be asked: If necessity is thus ruled out, how can the will be obligated to act for an end? One is tempted to compare this statement of Anselm with Kant's statement that the precise difference between the hypothetical and the categorical imperative is that the hypothetical denotes that an act is necessary as a means to an end, whereas the categorical denotes an act as necessary in itself without any relation to any other end. Cf. *Immanuel Kant's Werke*, Vol. IV, *Grundlegung zur Metaphysik der Sitten* (Cassirer ed., Berlin, 1922), p. 271.

[10] *Loc. cit.* For the importance of the will in Anselm, see the brief account by J. Sheets, "Justice in the Moral Thought of St. Anselm," *The Modern Schoolman*, XXV (1948), 1932–39. On the development of the concept of *liberum arbitrium* in general, consult O. Lottin *Psychologie et morale aux XII e et XIII e siècles* (Louvain: Mt. César, 1942), chaps. 1–2.

The fact that these statements were made by Augustine and Anselm from the ascetical point of view and therefore admit of a correct interpretation, is one thing; the fact that they are used by others as a foundation for philosophical explanations of the nature of the intellect and will, is quite another.

says that, that power is pre-eminent whose habit, act, and object are pre-eminent. But this is true of the will. Therefore the will is the pre-eminent power.[11]

The proof of this statement lies first, says Henry, in the fact that the habit of charity—than which there is no greater—resides in the will.[12] Henry here cites Augustine,[13] thereby showing, as was mentioned, one of the principal sources of his own inspiration.

The second reason why the will is superior, according to Henry, is that its acts are superior. That which is always acting and moving is nobler than that which is acted upon.[14] The will is that which first moves itself as well as other powers of the soul and as such is superior to all others, including the intellect.[15] In fact, the intellect, because it is concerned with particular ends, is contained under the will, which is concerned with the universal end. Hence it is the will which "moves, impels, and directs reason." [16]

Here for the first time we find Henry attributing to the will the act of directing—an act that implies a knowledge of the relation of means to end. Others later, such as Scotus and Suarez, will do the same thing. If there is any doubt whether Henry means this literally, we can be assured that he does. For, in explaining that that which directs is su-

---

[11] *Aurea quodlibeta,* Quodl. I, q.14, f. 17r, A-B.

[12] *Ibid.,* D.

[13] The reference which Henry gives is *De Trinitate,* Lib. XIV.

[14] *Ibid.,* C. Here Henry refers to Augustine, *De Genesi ad litteram,* XII, and *De libero arbitrio,* III; Aristotle, *De anima,* III; Anselm, *Liber de similitudinibus.*

[15] *Ibid.,* A.

[16] *Ibid.,* f. 17v, B-C.

perior to that which is directed, he says that directing can be of two kinds. Either it can be on the part of one in authority, such as the master directing the servant to do something. Here the master directing is clearly the superior. It is in this way that the will directs the intellect. Or directing can be on the part of one who is ministering, such as a servant who carries a light before the master. In this case such direction on the part of the servant is inferior because the master can cease to follow the servant whenever he wishes and may proceed on his own. This is the way the intellect directs the will. The will, if it wishes, can withdraw from the direction of the intellect and *"by its own power of knowing can direct itself."* [17]

With this startling statement the full nature of the will begins to appear. Besides being the source of all movement, it can also know and direct, acts which even Henry admits are also acts of the intellect. The will, like the master, is capable of everything the servant is capable of, and more. It is autonomous. It is practically a supposit by itself. It can be placed under no necessity by the intellect presenting the good. If it should be objected that the intellect must causally enter into any action of the will by presenting the good known, Henry still keeps the will independent by responding that it is not reason knowing which moves the will, but the good known. [18]

The way is now open for the will, when considered later as that of the lawgiver, not only to move but to direct.

---

17 *Ibid.*, D (italics added).
18 *Loc. cit.*

What is more, it need not now be necessitated to act according to what the intellect presents as objectively necessary for the attainment of the end.

The third reason why Henry believes that the will is superior is that its object and the manner of its attainment are superior. The object of the will is the good taken absolutely, and as such has the nature of an absolute and ultimate end. The object of the intellect, however, is the true which has the nature of some good as known and hence as a subordinate end which is further ordered to another as to the ultimate end.[19] God is the highest possible object of either the intellect or the will, but the way the will attains God is higher than the way the intellect attains Him. For the will, since it is inclined to its object and is received in it, is perfected by its existence in the object. The intellect, on the contrary, receives its object into itself so that the object is perfected by its existence in the intellect. So in regard to God, the will is perfected more in possessing God by giving itself over to Him than the intellect is by receiving God into itself through knowing Him. For in giving itself over to God as the good, the will is in a way converted into Him inasmuch as it then exists in God.[20] Or to put it another way, the intellect possesses its object only as a disposition of itself, as light in the air is a disposition of the air. The object, however, of the will is in the will like a flame changing the will into itself and making them identical, as a flame in the air

[19] *Loc. cit.*
[20] *Summae quaestionum ordinariarum,* I, a.48, q.2, f. 30v, L-K.

changes the air into itself. Thus the will is one with the
object: it is immersed in it through love. This penetra-
tion can never be effected by the intellect, for "love enters
in, where knowledge remains without." In sum, it is
nobler to be converted into a noble object than to possess
that object simply by way of a disposition.[21]

The superiority of the will also appears in Henry's explanation of freedom. Although, as he says, the intellect is
free after a fashion, the will is much freer. This is true because the will is a faculty which produces the act through
which it acquires its object by virtue of a principle within
itself and without any impulse or retraction from another.
The intellect, on the other hand, is impelled and determined by the object in its first act of understanding and
it is also impelled to act or not to act by the will. Hence the
will is much freer than the intellect.[22] Therefore the relation between the intellect and the will is not one of mutual
causality, but the intellect is only a condition for the action of the will. Freedom is in the intellect "only as an
occasion." [23]

Command: of the will. With the role of superiority already conferred on the will by Henry for the various reasons given above, it is not surprising to find him adding
to the will's prerogatives the act of command.[24] For, he
says, command belongs to that power which is supreme

21 *Ibid.,* f. 32r, T.
22 *Aurea quodlibeta,* Quodl. XIV, q.5, f. 347v, C-D.
23 *Ibid.,* Quodl. I, q.15, f. 19v, D. Cf. Suarez below, chap. 6.
24 *Ibid.,* Quodl. IX, q.6, f. 86v, B.

and has free dominion. For Henry that power is, of course, the will. Henry defines command as the intimation to another of something to be done.[25]

Elaborating on why command should be attributed to the will rather than to the intellect, Henry adduces three reasons: from the standpoint of the one commanding, of the one commanded, and of the thing commanded.[26]

First, then, in regard to the one commanding. Whenever many things contribute to the constitution of one thing, one of the contributing causes must be regarded as principle.[27] And because, as has already been shown, the will is superior, it belongs to the will to command. For the will can act against reason; it can force it; it can withdraw from its judgment; it can prevail upon it to consent. True, the will cannot will what is unknown. Hence there is need of a previous act of the intellect which, by an intimative motion, inclines the will to command. This, however, is not the command but an act disposing in regard to the command, because by it the will is not at all fettered. Otherwise, if the will were fettered by this act, it would be more than mere motion: it would be compulsion, and command would then be of the intellect. So, because by this act the intellect only disposes the will to command, it had best be called only an order (*jussio*) and command should be reserved only for the will.[28] Here again it is obvious that Henry is averse to allowing the intellect any

---

[25] *Loc. cit.*

[26] It should be noted that this is the passage referred to by Suarez, *De legibus,* I, c.5, n.8.

[27] *Aurea quodlibeta,* Quodl. IX, q.6, f. 87r, A.

[28] *Ibid.,* f. 87r, D.

true causality in its action on the will. It can at most only dispose. Hence command must be of the will.

Secondly, in regard to the one commanded. The relation between the one commanded and the one commanding is such that the former must of necessity obey the latter.[29] This is the case in regard to all the other powers and the will. They must all of necessity obey the will.[30] Hence, once again, command can be an act only of the will.

Thirdly, in regard to the thing commanded. What is comanded, Henry says, is an act to be performed by the one receiving the command. No command is ever given if the act to be executed does not fall within the competency of the one expected to do it. But no other power can command the will in regard to its own act. Only the will can command itself. Therefore only "the will can command, not the intellect." [31]

II

Henry of Ghent seems to have made no attempt to state explicitly the essence of law in terms of the psychological principles he had already established, as others did later. However, two things he did treat in regard to law which show implicitly what he considered the essence of law and its psychological implications, namely, the foundation of obligation and the nature of pure penal law.

Law and obligation. In regard to obligation Henry asks: Why is a subject obliged to obey? He answers that subjects

29 *Ibid.*, f. 87v, D.
30 *Ibid.*, f. 87r, D.
31 *Ibid.*, f. 88r, D-f. 88v, A. Cf. *ibid.*, Quodl. I, q. 14, f. 17r, C.

are obliged to obey their superiors in regard to those things which are for the common welfare.[32] Why is this true? Because the end intended by the prince or prelate is the peace and well-being of the commonwealth which the individual subjects are also obliged to intend, since they are parts of the community.[33] Henry then proceeds to give an explanation of the foundation of obligation which, at first sight, seems to be in terms of objective finality, but which ultimately turns out to be quite otherwise. Because, he says, means to an end derive their necessity from the end for which they are necessary, if one is obliged to intend the end so also is one obliged to intend the means necessary to attain the end and to place acts that will be ordered to the end. Therefore, since it is the part of princes and superiors to determine (*ordinare*) in these matters what, when, and how means are necessary for the end, every subject is obliged to obey the statutes set up by superiors in regard to means necessary for the end. This is true in regard to those things without which the end could not be attained at all, as well as in regard to those things without which it could not be attained conveniently.[34] Hence, once again, subjects are obliged to obey the statutes of superiors which are for the common welfare.[35]

Does this mean that the foundation for obligation is the objective relation between the means considered in their very nature and the common good, which relation the superior cannot determine, but only take account of and

32 *Ibid.,* Quodl. XIV, q.8, t.2, f. 352r, B.
33 *Ibid.,* C.
34 *Loc. cit.*
35 *Ibid.,* f. 352v, A.

judge accordingly; or does it mean that the foundation for obligation is subjective, the will of the superior determining what means shall be placed, not primarily because the means of their nature may or may not contribute to the common good and the superior is thereby necessitated to so judge, but simply because it is his prerogative to so will? Henry has just said that it is the office of the prince or superior to ordain in these matters "how they are necessary for the attainment of the end." [36] This seems to indicate that he favors the latter opinion. But such a vague and general statement hardly warrants a definite conclusion. We must seek more conclusive evidence.

Purely penal law. Such evidence is unmistakably furnished when Henry asks the question: Do all laws oblige in conscience to that which is commanded? [37] Is the foundation of obligation such that the lawgiver has no choice whether the law will oblige in regard to the thing commanded? Or is it such that he may will and intend that the law oblige, not in regard to the thing commanded, but only in regard to the payment of the penalty? Henry's answer is that there may be laws which oblige only to the payment of the penalty if the lawgiver so wills. Why? Because the source and foundation of obligation is the will of the lawgiver.

Let us see how Henry arrives at this conclusion. First he

---

[36] *Loc. cit.*

[37] *Ibid.*, Quodl. III, q.22, t. 1, f. 129v. This seems to be one of the earliest attempts to explain and justify philosophically the theory of purely penal law. Castro says Henry was one of the early authors who developed this idea, and Suarez refers to him as one of the *antiqui* who held this position.

assures us that what the legislator primarily intends is the observance of the law and the doing of good deeds. Any penalty that may be attached is intended only secondarily: to spur on the obstinate.[38] Hence every law with a penalty attached obliges in conscience somehow. But when and how? [39]

This depends on how a penal law, that is, one with a penalty, is instituted. It may be instituted in one of two ways. It may be instituted as a double statute with one legal and one penal statute. For instance, in a religious order there may be a statute that "no one should speak after Compline," which is a legal statute. Immediately there is added that, "if one does speak after Compline, he must say the seven penitential psalms." This is the penal statute. In this manner of legislating, Henry says, the legal statute is principal. It does not depend upon the second or penal statute. Rather, of itself, it obliges in conscience, both because of its form and because of the fact that the intention of the lawgiver is that it so oblige.[40]

The other way in which a law may be instituted is as one single penal statute. For instance, again in a religious order, there could be a statute in this form: "Whoever speaks after Compline shall say the seven penitential psalms." Now, in such a statute two things are to be considered: the form of the statute and the intention of the lawgiver. As to the form, it is obvious that what is primarily legislated is the penalty, and the observance on

[38] *Ibid.*, Quodl. III, q. 22, t. 1, f. 130r, C.
[39] *Ibid.*, D.
[40] *Loc. cit.*

account of which the penalty is imposed in no way is included in the form of the statute. Therefore such a penal law, considered as to its form, says Henry, "obliges only to the payment of the penalty and in no way in conscience" to the observance of what is commanded. With regard to the intention of the lawgiver, this may be to bring about observance indirectly through restraint or fear, so that acts which are in themselves bad will never occur or so that acts which are indifferent in themselves but forbidden by the superior will happen less frequently.[41] Hence, since it is the intention of the lawgiver, such a penal statute obliges in conscience only to the payment of the penalty, not to the thing commanded. For "in such a case the penalty is sustained without fault, though not without cause." [42] From this passage it seems safe to conclude that the foundation of obligation is, for Henry, the will—the intention of the lawgiver.

Why is it that never once does Henry attempt to solve this problem of penal law in terms of finality: in terms of the objective necessity of means (silence after Compline) to the end (the common good of the religious community)? Why did he not apply what even he himself had said in regard to the means deriving their necessity from the end? [43]

At the very least, it can be said that the idea of finality

[41] *Ibid.*, f. 131r, A-C. Henry's inclusion under the matter of law of what was good or bad in itself as well as what was indifferent, was later repeated, as we shall see, as a basis for distinguishing between what was necessary and what was only useful, and for distinguishing between laws that obliged in conscience to what was commanded and laws that obliged only to the payment of the penalty. Cf. below, Scotus, chap. 2, note 62.

[42] *Ibid.*, C. This distinction between *sine culpa* and *sine causa* will be encountered again in Castro; cf. below chap. 5.

[43] Cf. above, p. 18.

was not a principle operative in Henry's thought when he attempted to solve these problems. What could be the reason for this? Is he consistent? The reason for it and the basis for his consistency are one and the same: his philosophy of intellect and will. Henry had said that the command is of the will. If this is so, then obligation, which derives from command, must also be founded on the will and intention of the lawgiver. This seems to have been the guiding principle in the back of Henry's mind when he wrote on purely penal law.

Attention must be called at this juncture to a point of the utmost importance in the history of the development of this question. Henry of Ghent, as did (and do) many others, takes for granted that the meaning of law, which includes the source of authority and basis of obligation, in the civil union is analogous to that of the religious union. In fact he says: "In this matter I see no difference between the relation of clerics or laymen to their superiors." [44] This assertion has been flatly denied. Cajetan, Soto, Medina, and Bellarmine say that if the word "law" is to be used in regard to religious unions, its meaning is absolutely equivocal.[45]

Henry of Ghent, then, is a man of great importance in the development of this question. He was often quoted (as we shall see) in the centuries that followed as the great proponent of the primacy of the will. Command was an act

[44] *Ibid.*, f. 352r, C; cf. *ibid.*, f. 131r, D. Cf. also, for instance, below: Castro, chap. 5, and Suarez, chap. 6.
[45] Cf. below: chap. 9, p. 155; chap. 10, p. 175; chap. 11, p. 193; chap. 12, p. 216.

of the will. Hence law was an act of the will. Because the will was free from any physical necessity on the part of the intellect, so also was it free from any moral necessity thence imposed. Therefore the foundation of obligation had to be the will itself.

CHAPTER II

JOHN DUNS SCOTUS

I

JOHN DUNS SCOTUS, O.F.M. (1266–1308) [1] with great clarity saw that the heart of this question was: What is the nature of the will? He taught at Oxford in 1300 and at Paris in 1302, and was greatly influenced by the previous condemnations of 1270 and 1277. For him, as for many others of his generation, these events were powerful and decisive factors in determining their approach to the problem of the nature of intellect and will.

It was easy to see where the Greek necessitarianism of Aristotle, as embodied in Averroism and Thomism, led: to a denial of liberty in man and in God. Now, in this position the intellect was the prime faculty, and it was the intellect's necessitating influence on the will that led to such disastrous results. Consequently Scotus' work was cut out for him: to save liberty by vindicating the primacy of the will. [2]

---

[1] St. Bonaventure (1221–74) was not included here because his treatment of this matter is not as full or as important as Scotus'.

[2] For the life and works of Duns Scotus, see Mariano F. Garcia, O.F.M., *De vita et doctrina B. Joannis Duns Scoti* (7th ed.; Quaracchi, 1914); also Bernard Landry, *Duns Scot* (Paris: Alcan, 1922). On the supremacy of the will in Scotus, consult Paul Vignaux, *Justification et prédestination au XIV e siècle* (Paris: Leroux, 1934), chap. 1.

Will is primary. For Scotus, then, the will was man's greatest power, his "most noble perfection." [3] As a matter of fact, the will was a principle that was uniquely distinct from all others.[4] Why was the will nobler than the intellect? Because—as Augustine, Anselm, and Henry of Ghent had said before him—charity is a habit of the will and it is more perfect than either faith or hope, as the apostle Paul had pointed out.[5] Charity perfects the will and makes it just; this truth is the basis for our friendship with God.[6] Then, too, that power is primary which has the principal part in beatitude. This obviously is the will. Hence the will is primary.[7] With such emphasis on charity and love of God, it is not surprising that Scotus' first practical principle was one that pertained to the will: Love God.[8]

Thus for Scotus the will, and not the intellect, was man's noblest perfection because it was precisely this which distinguished him from the brutes. Man is essentially different from the brute because his will is not moved by natural necessity.[9] The distinction, therefore, between nature and liberty, between intellect and will, is radical. Each has its own proper way of acting. The intellect acts after the manner of nature. The will has a unique mode of action, it acts freely.[10] Whereas the intellect is moved by an object

3 *Reportata Parisiensia,* II, d.25, n.3, 17. In 1639 an *Opera omnia* was edited by Wadding at Lyons. This was reprinted by Vivés in Paris, 1891–95.

4 *Metaph.,* IX, q.15, n.8.

5 *Commentaria Oxoniensia,* IV, d.49, q.4. A critical edition of the first two books of this *Commentary* has been published by Garcia at Quaracchi, 1912–14.

6 *Ibid.,* III, d.26, n.18; cf. *ibid.,* d.34, n.17; *ibid.,* IV, d.49, q.5, n.3.

7 *Rep. Par.,* IV, q.3, n.7.

8 *Comm. Oxon.,* IV, d.46, q.1, n.10.

9 *Quodl.,* q.21, n.14.

10 *Ibid.,* q.16, n.13; cf. *Oxon.,* IV, d.49, q.10, n.2; *Oxon.,* I, d.1, q.4; *Quodl.,* q.16, n.4.

with natural necessity, the will freely moves itself.[11] In other words, the intellect elicits its act necessarily and is determined by its intelligible object; whereas the will is completely indetermined and is not necessitated in any way by the intellect, in regard either to specification or to exercise.

Hence the intellect is not allowed a true causal part in the action of the will. Its function is limited to that of a condition. "Nothing but the will is the total cause of willing." [12] "For the act of willing, nothing except the will is required." [13] The will itself is the adequate cause of its determination.[14] If it should be objected that the determining of the will to act or not must be on the part of the intellect representing the object, Scotus answers that this cannot be the case. If this were so, it could only be because the intellect cannot determine the will indifferently to one of two contradictories except by demonstrating the one and paralogizing or reasoning sophistically in regard to the other, so that there would be deception in the conclusion. Therefore, if that contingency by which the will acts or does not act should be from the intellect dictating according to the above conclusion, then, according to this, nothing would contingently proceed from the will of God, because He neither paralogizes nor deceives.[15] Hence

---

[11] *Quodl.*, q. 16, n. 6; cf. *Oxon.*, IV, d. 46, q. 1, n. 10–11.

[12] *Oxon.*, II, d. 25, n. 22; cf. *Rep. Par.*, II, d. 25, n. 20. Cf. below, Suarez, chap. 6.

[13] *Quodl.*, q. 21, n. 13–17; cf. *Metaph.*, IX, q. 15.

[14] H. de Montefortino, *Venerabilis Johannis Duns Scoti summa theologica ex universis operibus eius concinnata* (Rome, 1900), I, q. 83, a. 1; cf. *Rep. Par.*, I, d. 10, q. 3, n. 4. Cf. Henry of Ghent, above, chap. 1.

[15] *Oxon.*, II, d. 25, n. 23.

"nothing is so much in the power of the will as the will itself." [16] Indeed, the will alone is supreme.[17]

That the essence of the will consists, for Scotus, in its complete freedom and indetermination from any necessity coming from outside itself and in its power to choose between opposite alternatives [18]—and not in a necessary inclination to the good in general—is shown by his explicit rejection of the Aristotelian principle (and Thomistic, for that matter, too) that, as the intellect necessarily assents to first principles in the order of speculation, so also the will necessarily assents to the ultimate end in the order of action.[19] The will can will the end freely, in general as well as in particular.[20] Unless this is admitted, he says, we are immediately confronted with many fallacies. Thus the conclusion would have to be admitted that, just as we assent to a necessary conclusion on account of principles, so also we "would have to assent necessarily to those means which lead to an end on account of the end." This, he says, is false.[21] It is false because, first, the will does not necessarily follow that order in its acts which things that can be willed have of their nature. Nor, secondly, is assent here similar. For there is necessity in the intellect deriving from the evidence of the object necessarily causing this assent in the intellect, but the goodness of the object does

---

[16] *Ibid.*, d.7, n.23; cf. *Quodl.*, q.16, n.4. This is a quotation from Augustine, *Retract.*, I, c.22.

[17] *Rep. Par.*, IV, d.49, q.2, n.6.

[18] *Quodl.*, q.18, n.9.

[19] *Oxon.*, I, d.1, q.4, n.2. This is quoted by St. Thomas, *Sum. theol.*, I–II, q.90, a.1, c; cf. also *ibid.*, I, q.82, a.1, c; I–II, q.8, a.2, c.

[20] *Oxon.*, IV, d.49, q.10, n.9.

[21] *Ibid.*, I, d.1, q.4, n.2. Cf. *ibid.*, II, d.7, n.27.

not necessarily cause the assent of the will. The will freely assents to any good, whether it be greater or less.[22]

In this capital passage one thing should be noted immediately. Scotus makes no distinction between physical necessity and moral necessity. When he says: "We would have to assent necessarily to those means which lead to an end on account of the end," he does not make it clear that in attacking Aristotle's and Thomas' principle on the point of physical necessity he is also throwing out their foundation for moral necessity. For, while it would be true that there would be no liberty if man were physically necessitated to choose means that led to an end, so also it is true (as, for instance, St. Thomas says) that there is no objective reason why he ought to choose them unless they are necessary for the end. Scotus' failure to clarify this point here, at least would indicate that the possibility of moral necessity being founded on objective finality had made little or no impression on him. The will itself was sufficient explanation.

So, concerning this Aristotelian proposition, Scotus continues that it is at most only a simile, namely: as the intellect, tending orderly to truth on account of principles, assents to the conclusion, so the will, tending orderly to what is the end, tends to it on account of the end. But there is no simile, he says, expressed by the proposition if there is question of comparing the powers, since the intellect is moved by the object with natural necessity, whereas the will freely moves itself. Moreover, there is no simile in regard to the necessity in question. For the con-

22 *Oxon.*, I, d.1, q.4, n.2.

clusion is known necessarily through the principle, but
means are not thus necessarily sought on account of the
goodness of the end.[23]

Scotus admits this is against those who (like Thomas)
held that the will necessarily wills the end, but not the
means to the end.[24] If you object that the will as nature
wills the end, but that as will it wills the means to the
end, Scotus replies that opposed ways of acting cannot be in the same power, especially the modes
"natural" and "free." Because, if the will is related
to the end naturally and to the means freely, it will not be
one active power in respect to these, and then there will
be no power at all which chooses means to the end on account of the end.[25] The will, therefore, considered as an
elicitive principle, would be both active and passive in
seeking the end. Therefore it would be both active and
passive under the same aspect, which is impossible.[26]

This basic distinction between nature and freedom
further serves as the foundation for the distinction between willing that which is satisfying or contributive to
happiness in general,[27] and willing that which is just and
to be sought in and for itself.[28] The inspiration here is, of
course, Anselmian.[29] As Scotus says, inasmuch as the will
is a mere natural intellectual appetite, it is inclined to

23 *Quodl.*, q. 16, n. 6.
24 *Oxon.*, II, d. 5, q. 2, n. 6.
25 *Ibid.*, I, d. 10, n. 10.
26 P. Minges, O.F.M., *Joannis Duns Scoti doctrina philosophica et theologica* (Quaracchi, 1930), I, 307. Cf. *Oxon.*, IV, d. 49, q. 10, n. 13.
27 *Oxon.*, III, d. 26, n. 21.
28 *Ibid.*, IV, d. 49, q. 4, n. 6.
29 *Ibid.*, II, d. 6, q. 2, n. 7. Cf., e.g., Anselm, *De concord. praesc. Dei cum
lib. arbit.*, cap. 13 (*PL*, CLVIII, 538); *De voluntate* (*PL*, CLVIII, 488).

seek whatever is satisfying; but inasmuch as the will is
free, it must control this natural appetite and act according to justice.[30] The action of the free will must be just
and right in order that its natural inclinations be con-
trolled.[31]

That justice is to be sought for its own sake is something
that received great stress in Anselm.[32] This fact was not
lost on Scotus. For justice was not to be willed as a means
to some end—even one's own perfection, it seems [33]—but
solely "in and for itself." [34] What is of the utmost importance here is that it is against the nature of the will to do
otherwise.[35] What distinguishes the will from all other
appetites is that it can will a good (even to another) on
account of the good itself only.[36] In other words, when the
will embraces a true good in and for itself, it acts in a
higher way than when it chooses on account of an end.
The basic reason why Scotus was led to speak thus seems
to be that in his mind it was only natural, like the brute,
to seek your own perfection and the satisfying (com-
modum) which led to it.[37] But it was to act in a way dis-

[30] *Oxon.*, II, d.6, q.2, n.8–9; cf. *ibid.*, d.25, n.23.
[31] *Rep. Par.*, II, d.23.
[32] Cf. above, chap. 1.
[33] *Oxon.*, IV, d.28, n.2–d.29, n.2. This statement should be compared with
that of St. Thomas in which perfection of self is clearly indicated as of the
metaphysical essence of love: ". . . for every man God will be the whole reason for loving inasmuch as God is the whole good of man. For if, by an impossible supposition, God were not the good of man, there would be no reason
for him loving" (*Sum. theol.*, II–II, q.26, a.13 ad 3).
[34] *Oxon.*, III, d.27, q.1, n.3. Cf. *Rep. Par.*, III, d.29, n.2; *Oxon.*, IV, d.49,
q.2, n.20.
[35] *Oxon.*, IV, d.49, q.2, n.22.
[36] *Ibid.*, q.5, n.6.
[37] *Ibid.*, q.10, n.3.

tinctly human, that is, freely, to seek not your own end but justice in and for itself.[38]

Command: of the will. With the will and its freedom so dominating Scotus' thought, the command could hardly be other than an act of the will. The intellect can command neither itself nor the will; whereas the will can command both the intellect and itself.[39] The reasons for this assertion seem to be, first, the will is the moving power. Hence all other powers of the soul must obey it.[40] The will, therefore, is independent of the judgment of reason and can move itself against it.[41] Secondly, command is of the will because the intellect in pointing out the truth can only incline to action, but the will can dictate that the thing be done.[42] This means that the intellect does not enter into the action of the will as a true cause. It is rather ordered to the act of the will.[43]

True, Scotus gives the end on account of which acts are chosen (for instance, *commoda*) its proper recognition; [44] but will it be the intellect that will be given the office of ordering these acts as means to the end? Again, as in Henry of Ghent, it will not. It is the will which orders.[45] If confirmation is needed regarding the full meaning of "order"

38 *Ibid.*, q.5, n.3. Cf. *ibid.*, III, d.26, q.1, n.17.
39 *Ibid.*, IV, d.14, q.2, n.5.
40 *Rep. Par.*, II, d.42, q.4, n.14.
41 *Oxon.*, IV, d.49, q.4, n.16.
42 *Ibid.*, d.14, q.2, n.5.
43 *Ibid.*, d.6, q.11, n.3.
44 *Ibid.*, I, d.1, q.2, n.14. Cf. *ibid.*, IV, d.6, q.5, n.2; *ibid.*, I, Prol., q.4, n.44.
45 *Ibid*, II, d.30, q.2, n.3.

(*ordinare*), Scotus will not hesitate to make one of the most radical statements in his psychology: "The will has the power of comparing *just as the intellect has* and as a consequence, when things are presented to it, it can make a comparison *as the intellect can*." [46] The will, therefore, is truly capable of ordering—thus implying the perception of a relation—means to an end.

With the will now capable of commanding and ordering, the foundation for Scotus' philosophy of law and obligation is well prepared.

II

Law: of the will. Scotus' definition of law does not immediately reduce law to its psychological essence, that is, whether it be an act of the intellect or of the will. He merely says in general that law is a practical truth proclaimed by one having authority.[47] Nor does the relation between law and obligation appear from his explanation that it is called law (*lex*) because it binds or obliges (*ligat*) those to whom it is given [48] and that it is for the common good.[49] That wisdom, prudence, and authority are required in the legislator,[50] still leaves the matter somewhat vague.

[46] *Ibid.*, d.6, q.1, n.6 (italics added). In view of such statements as this, it seems futile to defend the "intellectualism" of Scotus. Cf. Minges, *op. cit.*, I, 287.

[47] *Rep. Par.*, IV, d.15, q.4, n.9.

[48] *Loc. cit.*

[49] *Oxon.*, IV, d.14, q.2, n.7. Cf. *ibid.*, d.46, q.1, n.11; *Rep. Par.*, IV, d.15, q.4, n.10.

[50] *Rep. Par.*, IV, d.15, q.4, n.9. Cf. *Oxon.*, IV, d.15, q.2, n.6.

When, however, quoting Augustine, he says that no law is just unless it descends from the divine law as a practical conclusion from practical principles,[51] we are led to the divine law as possibly furnishing a clue to the answer we seek: the nature of law and obligation and its relation to Scotus' psychology.

Does divine law pertain to the divine intellect or to the divine will? Scotus is quite definite that divine law pertains to the divine will, which also, as we shall see, is the source of obligation.

Why does Scotus place divine law in the divine will? Because, true to his philosophy of intellect and will in general, the will, human or divine, cannot be put under any necessity by the intellect presenting intelligible essences. It must remain free to determine of itself what is right and true in the practical order. Hence, Scotus says, it is only the divine will which is capable of commanding what is to be done, and this is law. True, the intellect apprehends what is to be done before the will wills and commands it. But the divine intellect does not apprehend determinately "This is to be done," which would be to dictate or command. Rather, since the divine intellect is neutral or indifferent, it is the divine will that determines by its own willing the law: "This is to be done." The divine intellect then apprehends as true that this is to be done.[52] Further, just as a law is true if it is in conformity with the divine will, so it has its rectitude and order from the divine will.

51 *Oxon.*, IV, d.15, q.3, n.7.
52 *Ibid.*, d.46, q.1, n.10.

The rightness of a law depends upon its acceptance by the divine will.[53] Even justice itself is in direct dependence on the divine will.[54]

Obligation: from the will. Now, if the will can determine the rightness of a law, is this not the same as saying that the will can determine the order of means to an end? Can the will determine the necessity of means over and above that which would seem to follow from the very essence of the means? In a word, what for Scotus is the foundation of obligation?

In explaining the relation of means to end Scotus says that a person may be turned away from the ultimate end in one of two ways: either formally by explicitly rejecting the end, or virtually by rejecting the means which are necessary to attain the end, thereby virtually rejecting the end.[55] The first way of turning away from the end, that is, formally, is a special sin, hatred of God. The latter way of turning from the last end, that is, virtually, is common to all mortal sin, the rejection of a means necessary for the end. Scotus now asks the important question: What is the reason why certain means may be necessary? One possible answer would be that, created essences being what they are (the creative act being therefore presupposed), human acts of their very nature have a necessary relation to man's end and that necessity must be founded upon this relation. To say this, however, would be contrary to the freedom from essences as presented by the intellect, a

53 *Ibid.*, I, d. 44, q. 1, n. 2.
54 *Ibid.*, IV, d. 46, q. 1, n. 7–12.
55 *Ibid.*, II, d. 37, q. 1, n. 8.

freedom that Scotus has already given to the will. Hence the only consistent response for him is to say that necessity comes only "from the divine command willing that certain acts be performed." [56] The foundation of obligation, therefore, in Scotus is the divine will.

That the divine precept which Scotus speaks of is a positive precept (and not the creative act of the divine will, which could broadly be called a precept) is shown by what he says concerning the foundation of necessity or obligation in the Decalogue, which is divine positive precept. Although in regard to those acts which are concerned with the end formally and which are expressed in the first table of the Decalogue, Scotus is willing to say that they have a necessary relation to the end, nevertheless in regard to all other acts, that is, those virtually connected with the end (the means to the end), which are expressed in the second table, he insists that any necessary relation they have to the end comes only from the divine precept. For instance, "adultery and murder in themselves would not be sins if God should revoke the precept." [57] The fact that, man's essence being what it is, these acts would of their very nature be contrary to it and therefore bad, does not mean that for that reason he would be necessitated or obliged to avoid them. Man's end could be attained through these acts if they were not positively forbidden.[58]

In other words, although man's intellectual nature may indicate which acts are good or bad, the necessity or obligation to place or omit them must come from another

[56] *Loc. cit.*
[57] *Ibid.,* IV, d.50, q.2, n.10.
[58] *Ibid.,* III, d.37, n.5–8.

source. It must come from the positive precept and command of the divine will. In sum, although man's nature may be a *lex indicans,* it is not a *lex obligans.*[59] The good act is not necessarily a right act. The good act is so because of a relation to nature. A right act implies something different, a relation to end.[60] Ockham and Biel would soon repeat this same distinction, as would many others during the succeeding six hundred years.[61]

Even Scotus' basis for distinguishing between mortal and venial sin is not primarily in terms of relation of the act to the end: whether the act makes the attainment of the end absolutely impossible or only impedes progress toward it. His basis for distinguishing is in terms of precept and counsel. If an act comes under a precept and for that reason is necessary for the attainment of the end, its omission is mortal. If, on the other hand, the act does not come under a precept, but is only a matter of counsel and therefore is only useful in reaching the end, then its omission is only venial.[62]

Having made the necessity of certain means for the end

[59] As Montefortino commenting on Scotus says, the principles of the natural law "do not have the force of a law which obliges, unless there is an act of the will commanding that they be done" (*op. cit.,* II, q.94, a.1 ad 1, p. 609).

[60] Compare the opposite opinion of St. Thomas (*Sum. theol.,* I–II, q.21, a.1).

[61] Cf. below, Ockham, chap. 3; Biel, chap. 4; Suarez, chap. 6.

[62] *Oxon.,* II, d.21, q.1, n.3; cf. *Rep. Par.,* II, d.21, q.1, n.3. It should be noted that Scotus' distinction between necessary and useful, though not felicitous as a basis for distinguishing mortal and venial sin, is well taken in regard to precept and counsel. If a precept or law is concerned only with what is somehow necessary for the common good, then that which is only useful is not the matter of law as such. Failure to realize this has resulted in later authors including both what is necessary and what is useful under strict law, with the consequence that laws which commanded what was necessary were said to oblige to what was commanded, and laws which commanded what was only useful were said to oblige only to the payment of the penalty.

depend upon divine precept, it is only consistent for Scotus to declare that a large number of acts which do not come under any precept are indifferent, not only in the abstract but also in the concrete. Hence a large number of acts are neither meritorious nor demeritorious. They are supernaturally indifferent.[63] Acts could actually be placed which have no relation to man's last end, the beatific vision. Here Scotus sets up the distinction between a philosophical and a theological fault. A man might sin against the demands of his intellectual nature. This would simply be against reason and therefore a philosophical sin. Only if a positive divine precept were violated would it be a matter of true morality and therefore a theological sin. In human action the line between the philosophical and the theological is, for Scotus, sharp and distinct.[64] The stage was gradually being set for the controversy on the *peccatum philosophicum* [65] that followed some three centuries later. The two currents of thought which met head on during this controversy still show themselves in the various attempts now being made to solve the problem of the relation of moral philosophy to moral theology.

In Scotus, then, we have the metaphysics of the primacy of the will brought to its highest development. Just as in

[63] *Ibid.*, d.41, n.4. Cf. *Quodl.*, q.18, n.9; also Bonaventure, *In II Sent.*, d.41, a.1, q.3, Resp. (Quaracchi ed.), II, 944 and ad 5, p. 945; also *ibid.*, q.2, Resp., p. 940.

[64] *Ibid.*, d.37, q.1, n.8.

[65] As Montefortino explains, commenting on Scotus: ". . . whatever would be represented as against the judgment of reason would be considered an evil, not moral or theological but only natural and philosophical. For it would be against the dictate of reason, but it would not be against the law commanding and forbidding. Therefore it would be an evil against nature, but not a moral evil" (*op. cit.*, II, q.91, a.1, ad arg., p. 590).

his psychology the will is free from any necessity imposed by intelligible essences and liberty is exclusively of the will, so in law the will of the lawgiver is not ultimately determined or necessitated by the objective relation of means to end, and obligation comes from the act of the will commanding. If Scotus had written on penal law, it would have been only consistent for him to say that the lawgiver could will to oblige in conscience or not, as he saw fit, since all obligation comes from the will.

CHAPTER III

WILLIAM OCKHAM

I

WILLIAM OCKHAM, O.F.M. (1299–1349) was a man of extensive influence, as is attested by the followers he has had and the number of schools in which his doctrine was taught.[1]

Ockham taught at Oxford from 1312 to 1320 and followed Scotus (though he opposed him on many points), and the Franciscan tradition in general, in regard to the primacy of the will and the meaning of law. But there was a particular reason why he was led to assume this position. It was his theory of universals. For Ockham, the universal had no reality outside the mind. What actually existed outside the mind was only the individual. The universal, then, was only a term in the mind that signified the object of which it took the place, or for which it substituted in a proposition. This function of the term in taking the place of the object Ockham called "supposition."[2]

[1] For details of the life, works, editions, and general philosophic position of Ockham, consult P. Boehner, *The History of the Franciscan School*, Part IV, *William Ockham* (mimeograph, Detroit: Duns Scotus College, 1946). Boehner maintains that the name is William Ockham, and not William of Ockham (*op. cit.*, p. 1). On the primacy of the will in Ockham, see Paul Vignaux, *Justification et prédestination au XIVe siècle* (Paris: Leroux, 1934), chap. 3, pp. 127–40.

[2] For a brief account of Ockham's doctrine on this point, see S. C. Tornay, *Ockham: Studies and Selections* (La Salle, Ill.: Open Court Publishing Co., 1938).

The obvious consequence of such a theory of supposition is the nullification of the value of objective essences. Applied to the moral order, this meant that human acts have no definite objective essence: they are not good or bad by their very nature. And since, in the absence of objective essences which would be participations of the divine ideas, the divine intellect could not be the source of morality, this source had to be the divine will.[3]

Will more noble. Ockham's approach, then, to the question of which is the nobler faculty is through his philosophy of signification. Ockham held that the powers of the soul were really identical with the essence of the soul.[4] For, what is meant by the word "intellect" is the substance of the soul as being able to know, and the word "will" merely describes the substance of the soul as being able to will.[5] Thus there is one substance of the soul having acts distinct in reason alone, which therefore can have different denominations. When the soul elicits the act of knowing, it is called intellect; and when it elicits the act of willing, it is called will.[6] So, if it is said that the intellect is the nobler power, it is true; if it is said that the will is the nobler power, that is true also. For they are both in no way distinct, either in reality or in reason. Intellect and will are only words or names that connote distinct acts of knowing and willing.[7]

---

[3] Professor Gilson says: "The moment we radically suppress essences and universal archetypes, there remains no barrier that can restrain the arbitrariness of the divine power" (*La philosophie au moyen âge* [Paris: Payot, 1947], p. 652).
[4] *Super quatuor libros sententiarum* (Lyons, 1495), II, q. 24, K.
[5] *Loc. cit.*
[6] *Loc. cit.*
[7] *Ibid.*, I, d. 1, q. 2, K.

However, Ockham is willing to say that, granting the above distinction between the acts of knowing and of willing, then the will is the nobler power.[8] Why should this be so? Because the act of loving which is connoted by the will, is nobler than the act of knowing which is connoted by the intellect. Of course it could be conceded that the intellect is prior to the act of willing which is connoted by the will. So the act of knowing is a partial efficient cause with respect to the act of willing. It can exist naturally without the act of the will, but the act of the will cannot be without the act of the intellect. It should be borne in mind, however, says Ockham, that such priority on the part of the intellect does not imply that it is more perfect than the will.[9]

With the will thus receiving the honor of being the nobler faculty because it connotes the act of love, Ockham proceeds to draw the basic distinction between nature and will, as Scotus had done. The necessity of nature is completely opposed to liberty. Nature and the will are active principles having opposite ways of action. What is the principal reason for this? The will freely wills the end, whereas nature must incline to it with natural necessity. Proof that the will freely wills the end is that it is the same power which wills the end and the means to the end. Hence it must have the same manner of acting, because diverse modes of acting argue diverse powers. But the will acts freely in regard to means to the end. Therefore it acts freely in regard to the end itself.[10]

[8] *Loc. cit.*
[9] *Ibid.*, II, q.24, P.
[10] *Ibid.*, I, d.1, q.6, B. The verbatim similarity between this text and Scotus' *Oxon.*, I, d.1, q.4, is too obvious to be missed. Cf. Scotus above, chap. 2.

Ockham proceeds to elaborate on why the will can freely will the end, thereby indicating the importance he attaches to this point. The reason why the will can freely will the last end in general, he says, is because it is in its power to love happiness or not. It can seek happiness or not seek it. This is so because the will can refuse something if the intellect dictates that it should refuse it. But the intellect can believe that no happiness is possible, because it can believe that the only state possible is the one that we now *de facto* see. Therefore it can refuse everything that is contrary to the state which we now see, and as a consequence it can reject happiness.[11]

Ockham offers this confirmation. The will can refuse that in which it believes it would not be satiated. But it can believe that it would not be satiated in whatever is possible to itself. Hence it can refuse everything possible to itself. Now it is certain that it can reject whatever is impossible to itself. Therefore it can refuse whatever it wishes.

Besides, whoever can efficaciously will an antecedent, can will the consequent which is known and thought to be the consequent. But a person can efficaciously will not to exist and he can evidently know that not to be happy is a consequence of not existing. Therefore he can will not to be happy, and consequently he can refuse happiness. Ockham says that this is borne out by the facts. Many who have the use of reason—those who believe in a future life, as well as those who do not—kill themselves or expose themselves to dying. Therefore they will not to exist. Some who

11 *Ibid.*, P.

have the faith, knowing and believing they can attain happiness if they do not sin, choose to sin knowing and believing that on account of such sin they will receive eternal punishment. All this could not be possible unless it were possible for them to reject happiness, not only in general but also in particular.[12] Of course, like Scotus, Ockham admits that man has a natural inclination to his own perfection, but that does not mean that he has a natural inclination to his last end, happiness.[13]

The result of this metaphysics of will is the same as it was for Scotus. "Necessity of action" can come only from within the will as from "something intrinsic to an acting principle," and not from any objective relation between means and end that the intellect may present from intelligible essences.[14] Why? Because either the end moves and necessitates the will to act, or the will moves itself. But the end cannot move the will to act. If it did, there would be no freedom. The end does not necessarily move the will in regard to any created act. Therefore the will moves itself. It has no determination from the object.[15] It has only a greater or less approximation, which does not cause necessity. This is shown by the fact that a different approximation of the patient to the agent does not cause necessity of acting. It causes, at most, only more intense action, as in the case of a warm object and other objects to be warmed which are more or less proximate to it. But different potencies of an object (for instance, seen and not

12 *Loc. cit.*
13 *Ibid.,* X.
14 *Ibid.,* B.
15 There seems to be a contradiction between this and what Ockham says in regard to the act of knowing being a partial efficient cause of the act of willing.

seen) seem to be only a diverse approximation of the object of the act of the will to the will. Therefore it neither diversifies necessity nor causes necessity. It only makes the act more or less intense.[16] For these reasons, then, the will is put under no necessity of acting by the end.

Again it should be noted that, as in the case of Scotus, Ockham makes no distinction in this discussion between physical and moral necessity. The same criticism of it, therefore, must be made which was made in regard to Scotus' position.[17]

So, with respect to the interaction and intercausality of the intellect and will, Ockham says that if the will of necessity conforms to reason in eliciting its act, then it is no more free than the sense appetite. Because when there are two indifferent things which can be caused by diverse causes, if each of these things equally and with the same necessity is related to the causality of the diverse causes, each of them will be equally free. Now, granted the hypothesis that the will necessarily conforms to the reason when eliciting its act, then the will is indifferent to not willing and willing. With equal necessity it is related to the causality of the causes, just as the sense appetite is related to seeking and withdrawing from the object. Once the senses apprehend that this object is harmful or agreeable, the sense appetite immediately withdraws from it or seeks it. Nor can it resist. So, in like manner, if the will necessarily conforms to reason, then once the intellect judges that "this is to be done" or "this is to be avoided,"

16 *Loc. cit.*
17 Cf. p. 28 above.

immediately the will necessarily wills or does not will. This, of course, is obviously not the case. Hence the will is free from any necessity to follow the judgment of the intellect.[18]

Command: act of will. If the will is thus free to follow or not follow the judgment of the intellect, such a judgment is certainly not a command. Hence command cannot be an act of the intellect. It is an act of the will.

Because this conclusion was denied by many prominent adversaries, Ockham spares no effort in attempting to establish his position.

Hence he says, first, if you are going to hold that the command is an act of the intellect, regardless of how much you say the will can move the intellect, you must face this dilemma: either the intellect ultimately dictates that this command be chosen or it does not. If it does, the will necessarily conforms to the intellect by willing this command. Therefore the command is not in the power of the will, as the opposition would like to hold. Or, if the intellect does not dictate that the command be chosen by the will, then the will can will something that is not dictated by reason. This is also contrary to what the opposition would admit. Therefore—take it either way—it cannot be admitted that the intellect commands the will, nor can the will be said to be necessitated by it.[19]

Besides, as mentioned, the will no more depends upon the intellect in willing than the sense appetite does on

[18] *Ibid.*, III, q.12, a.4, 2, QQ.
[19] *Loc. cit.*

sense knowledge. The sense appetite can proceed to act, once the object has simply been presented, without any command from sense knowledge. Therefore all the more so can the will act without any command from the intellect.[20] It can act on its own command.

Besides, says Ockham still arguing the same point, either the intellect elicits its act necessarily or it does not. If it does, then in those things which are essentially so ordered that if one is placed the second must necessarily follow, the second is not in the power of the will unless the first is. But if the intellect dictates that such a command necessarily be elicited, it will necessarily be elicited. Hence this command is not in the power of the will. If the intellect does not elicit its act necessarily but freely, the same thing follows, namely, that the act of the intellect is first in the power of the will.[21]

Again, that command by which the will is said to impede the judgment of reason is an elicited act of the will. Hence it is conformed to right reason and not to this judgment of reason of which the command is destructive. For it is certain that if it were conformable to it, it would not be destructive of it. Therefore it is conformed to another judgment of reason, and concerning this judgment it may be asked, as in regard to the first, how it can be impeded by the command. This will not be by a command conformed to itself, because that command would be elicited conformable to right reason. Hence it must be impeded by some other command. This is also an act, and conse-

20 *Loc. cit.*
21 *Loc. cit.*

quently it necessarily conforms to some judgment of reason, but not to that judgment of which it is destructive, as is evident. Therefore it must conform to another prior judgment, and concerning this third judgment it can again be asked, as in regard to the first and the second, whence the judgment of reason can be impeded. Thus there will either be a process *in infinitum* of judgments and commands, or a stand must be taken in favor of some command which is not elicited in conformity to right reason but only freely upon the mere presentation of the object.[22]

Finally, the opposite position leads to the conclusion that the first sin was in the intellect and not in the will. For it consisted in that act which was first in our power. Consequently sin could not be voluntary. Now this, says Ockham, is against the teaching of Augustine and the saints. Confirmation comes from the fact that it does not seem impossible that God could suspend the action of a second cause, and cause a prior act without the posterior act. Hence He could cause that act of the intellect without the consequent act of the will. Thus sin would be in the intellect and not in the will.[23]

Thus, Ockham concludes, the opposite position is an untenable one. It is not the intellect which can command the will, but the will which can command the intellect.[24]

[22] *Loc. cit.*

[23] *Ibid.*, QQ-RR.

[24] *Ibid.*, QQ. It should be noted that in this entire passage the only judgment of reason that Ockham seems to have in mind is that of right reason or conscience. St. Thomas' *judicium electionis* (cf. below, chap. 8) seems to have escaped him entirely, as is to be expected in one who endows the will with the prerogative of autonomous action.

Ockham continues that if it should be said the will is not free because it can act against the judgment of reason, but it is free because it can freely command the execution of exterior operations and it is with respect to this command that it is called free, then that also is false. Because, when two things are so related that granted the first, the second necessarily follows, it is impossible that the first be present without the second following. Consequently the second is not in the power of the will unless the first is. But if right reason dictates what must absolutely be done and the will commands that it efficaciously be done, it necessarily is done and it is executed by the exterior powers if they are not impeded. Therefore the command of execution necessarily follows the command that it be done. Hence the will cannot be said to be free because it can freely command the execution after it has commanded that the act be done.[25]

Should it be asked whether to command the executive powers of the exterior act is a different act from that by which the will wills efficaciously the dictate of right reason, Ockham answers that you must make a distinction. If the act by which the dictate of right reason is willed is an imperative act formally (such, for instance, as is an act of heroic virtue), then it is absolutely one and the same act by which the will wills the dictate of right reason and commands the execution. For, once the former is placed the latter follows immediately, providing there is no impediment. If, however, the act is imperative only equivalently (for instance, if someone should will the dictate of reason

[25] *Ibid.*, RR.

and if, after having commanded the execution of the exterior act upon the opportunity, there should be an impediment), then in such a case there are two different acts. Here the first act is imperative only equivalently, the second formally. The first has an impediment for its object, the second does not. The second has the present time for its object, the first does not. Consequently there is question here of two different acts.[26]

It is of capital importance to mark here that Ockham, in the above critique, takes command as *one* act which has as its object both the election of prudence which implies a relation to the judgment of right reason (conscience) and the command which implies a relation to the external executive powers. Suarez, referring to this very passage, takes this position of Ockham on the command.[27] By way of comparison, for St. Thomas, as we shall see later, there is question here of *two acts* because there are two separate objects: one which is concerned principally with the decision of acting or not acting (the judgment of election of prudence); the other which is concerned with the ordering (*ordinare*) of the external powers (the command). For St. Thomas the command is an act of the intellect which follows the election and looks to the ordering of the execution of means to the end.[28] The possibility, however, of order and finality being of the essence of command is not according to Ockham's thought. For him, rather, the essence of command is intimately bound up with supremacy and motion of the will and its complete indetermina-

26 *Loc. cit.*
27 Cf. Suarez, *De leg.*, I, c. 5, n. 8. Cf. also below, chap. 6, note 19.
28 Cf. *Sum. theol.*, I–II, q. 17, a. 3 ad 1, and a. 1, c.

tion from any necessity imposed by the intellect. So the underlying reason for one or the other position is the part given to order, finality, and ensuing necessity in the operation of the will.

II

Law and obligation. Ockham's approach to law shows the impact of his psychology. For him, as we have just seen, the will is not to be placed under any necessity by essences or end. The objective nature of things does not determine the will's action.

Consistently then, Ockham says that a law is something which obliges one to avoid or do certain acts that are bad or good "because they are prohibited or commanded." [29] If this is Ockham's conception of law, immediately a question arises: Does this mean that, for Ockham, the goodness and badness of acts comes from the will of the lawgiver commanding that the acts be done or not done, and not from the relation between the objective essence of the act and the end of man? Does it mean that, consequently, obligation is founded on the will commanding, and not on the necessity of the act as means to the end? The former seems to be true in each case.

Ockham, like Scotus, discusses these problems principally in regard to the divine will. Is the divine will in any way necessitated or obligated by the divine essence—the divine ideas? Ockham answers, it is not. "By the very fact that God wills it, an act becomes good and just." [30] The

[29] *Quodlibeta septem,* Quodl. II, q. 14.
[30] *Sent.,* I, d. 17, q. 3, F; cf. *ibid.,* IV, q. 8–9, E.

goodness or badness of an act is determined by the will.
Likewise in regard to obligation. It proceeds directly from
the divine will commanding. In fact, he says, if God should
command one person and not another, the first would be
obliged and the second would not. The first would be
liable to sin, the second would not.[31] Man is obliged to will
what God wills that he should will.[32]

Further reasons for Ockham's centering law and obligation in the will alone are yielded by an analysis of his metaphysics—or lack of it—of essences and end. If there is any
doubt that Ockham is attempting to liberate the will from
all necessity deriving from natures and their relation to
end, it is dispelled by what he says concerning the hatred
of God. Hatred of God is considered by most authors to be
"intrinsically" evil, that is, of its very essence it is opposed
to the end of man. Ockham does not share this opinion.
Not only such things as stealing and adultery but even
hatred of God Himself "can become meritorious if they
come under a divine precept, just as now their opposite
comes under divine precept." [33] All that is needed is an
act of the divine will. God can cause such acts as hatred of
Himself because the "essence" of an act has no necessary
relation of conformity to or difformity from the end.[34]

Further light is thrown on Ockham's conception of the
relation of the "essence" of an act to the end when he says
that, if the hatred of God were caused by God alone, it
would always be on account of a good end, because God in

---

[31] *Ibid.*, IV, q.8–9, E.
[32] *Ibid.*, III, q.13, O.
[33] *Ibid.*, II, q.19, O. Cf. Bellarmine's opinion below, chap. 12.
[34] *Ibid.*, F; cf. *ibid.*, P. St. Thomas, *Sum. theol.*, I–II, q.21, a.1, constitutes
an interesting comparison.

no way can be injured by the hatred of a creature.[35] In other words, God could cause an act in man which would be essentially—intrinsically—opposed to the very end for which God created him. When Ockham does face the difficulty that the objective end of every act must be considered because there is an essential relation between the act and its end, he replies with two answers which are in regard to subjective aspects of the question and which therefore fail to meet the main difficulty: the objective necessity of end in every human act. He says first (having the dictum in mind: *Bonum ex integra causa, malum ex quocumque defectu*) that not every defect of circumstance required for a morally good act makes the act bad and a sin. For instance, a defect of knowledge—ignorance—excuses, as the doctors and saints agree. Secondly, he says that if there is a defect of some circumstance of the act that you are obliged to place, then its omission makes the act bad. But if you are not obliged to place such a circumstance (as, for instance, the end), then the act is not bad.[36]

Ockham's determination to keep the end from entering into the constitution of the human act as an actual cause is shown by his description of how an act is morally constituted good or bad by the end through extrinsic denomination only. Thus if an act which is morally indifferent is placed on account of a good end, then it does not become a good act except by extrinsic denomination. Likewise in regard to an indifferent act now placed on account of a bad

[35] *Ibid.*, ad 5, Q.
[36] *Ibid.*, I, d. 1, q. 1, ante J; cf. *ibid.*, II, q. 19, ad 5, Q; *ibid.*, q. 3, ad concl. 4, MM. Cf. also Scotus above, chap. 2.

end.[37] If you should ask what goodness is added to the substance of the act which is called good by extrinsic denomination, the answer is: Absolutely nothing distinct from what the act is in itself. The word "good" is only a name that signifies an indifferent act which connotes a virtuous act of a perfect will as well as right reason, in conformity to both of which it is elicited. So it is in regard to all acts of man.[38] Ockham finally openly declares his hand by saying that "the goodness of an act is not on account of right reason or on account of the end or other circumstance. . . . It is solely on account of an act of the will itself." [39]

Ockham, then, continues the tradition of the primacy of the will. The will commands, not the intellect. Law is of the will because, as in Scotus, ultimately whatever the divine will wills, that is law. Hence obligation, the effect of law, must have its foundation in the command of the will.

Undoubtedly the way was made easier for Ockham to solve the problem of the relation between will and intellect, between objective essences and end, first by reducing —according to his theory of signification—all essences, even concrete, to mere names; and secondly by denying that there was a real distinction between the soul and its faculties and therefore between the intellect and will. Just as it is characteristic of the position which holds the

[37] *Ibid.*, III, q. 10, P.
[38] *Ibid.*, Q.
[39] *Ibid.*, R. Comparison should be made with St. Thomas' *Sum. theol.*, I–II, q. 18, where the human act is considered in its existential aspect of *plenitudo essendi*.

primacy of the intellect to acknowledge concrete essences for what they are existentially, so it seems to be characteristic of the position which holds the primacy of the will to do the very opposite.

CHAPTER IV

GABRIEL BIEL

I

GABRIEL BIEL (1425–95), the last important thinker of this period who followed Ockham, was one of the clearest and most concise exponents of nominalism. In fact, Biel gives as his express purpose the restatement of Ockham's teaching.[1] At Tübingen for ten years he taught the "modern theology," that is, Ockham's nominalism. Biel can therefore be considered an authentic interpreter of the thought of Ockham.

Biel's works also have an added significance. He taught only twenty years before Luther, who knew the writings of Biel very well. How great an effect Biel had on Luther's subsequent thought is difficult to determine. That he had a definite influence on Luther, however, is beyond doubt.[2]

"Will"—"Intellect." Following Ockham's theory of signification and supposition,[3] Biel holds that actually

---

[1] *Ephythoma pariter et collectorium circa quatuor sententiarum libros,* Prol., A, 3. For general information on Biel's life and works, see Ruch, "Biel," *Dictionnaire de théologie catholique,* II (1932), 814–25; "Biel," *Kirchenlexicon,* II (2nd ed., 1883), 804–8; Karl Werner, *Die Scholastik des späteren Mittelalters* (Vienna: Braumüller, 1887).

[2] Cf., for instance, Paul Vignaux, *Luther, commentateur des Sentences* (Paris: Vrin, 1935) for the influence of both Ockham and Biel on Luther in regard to the virtue of charity. See also K. Feckes, *Die Rechtfertigungslehre des Gabriel Biel und ihre Stellung innerhalb der nominalistichen Schule* (Münster, 1925); *Theologische Quartalschrift* (1925), pp. 50–76.

[3] Cf. above, chap. 3.

there is no distinction between the soul and its faculties. Therefore there is no real distinction between the intellect and the will. However, a distinction can be made according to the different meanings of the word "potency." It can first be taken as a complete description expressing what is meant by the word "potency"; or it can be taken secondly only for that which is denominated by the name or concept. The word "intellect" is the substance of the soul capable of knowing; the word "will" is the substance of the soul capable of willing. Or, if you wish, the word "form" can be substituted for substance. If the word "intellect" is taken in the first manner, then it stands for the soul knowing as well as for the act of knowing, that is, both the thing denominated and the thing denominating. Similarly, the "will" is taken for the soul denominated and for the act of the will denominating. "Intellect" taken in the second way stands only for the immediate principle of the act of knowing, which is the soul that knows, and not for the act of knowing. In like manner the "will" stands only for the principle of the soul and not for the act of willing. Both intellect and will, however, connote or formally signify the act of the soul—intellect, the act of knowing; will, the act of willing.[4]

Two conclusions follow. First, the potencies of the soul (intellect, memory, and will) taken in the first way are distinguished from one another and from the soul. Secondly, the potencies of the soul (intellect, memory, and will) taken in the second manner are not distinguished from the

[4] *Ibid.,* I, d. 16, q. 1, M-N.

soul or from one another, either in reality or in reason.[5]

The above distinction being granted, which could be said to hold the primacy, the intellect or the will? Biel immediately manifests his preference for that faculty in which the uniqueness of man, freedom, is to be found. That faculty is the will because freedom is in the will. Freedom is that power which has dominion over its acts. It cannot be forced. It has its act completely within its own power. Such is the will. As Augustine had said, Biel continues, nothing is so completely within our own power as the will itself.[6] Likewise, St. Bernard said that everything pertaining to man is free in regard to merit and judgment solely on account of the will. They are not free of themselves. Therefore the will alone is free in man.[7] Hence it was the prerogative of freedom in the will that caused Biel to consider it the prime power.

The reasons Biel gives in explanation of the will's freedom are not without importance in regard to our problem. Immediately, following Anselm,[8] he shows an inclination to define freedom in terms of an autonomous will, one that is no way necessitated by the intellect presenting means necessary for an end. Thus Biel defines *liberum arbitrium* as "the power of keeping rectitude of the will for the sake of rectitude itself." [9] What does this mean? It means, he says, the power of conforming to the first and uncreated

---

[5] *Loc. cit.*
[6] *Ibid.,* II, d. 25, q. 1, **H.**
[7] *Loc. cit.*
[8] Cf. above, chap. 1.
[9] *Ibid.,* **D**; cf. *ibid.,* **F.**

rectitude, inasmuch as of its very nature it is for the sake of rectitude itself. Rectitude of will is therefore conformity to the divine will. Or, to put it another way, it is the power of willing something conformable to the divine will.[10]

But now the important question: Why? Why should anyone will in conformity to the divine will? In other words, why is he necessitated or obliged? Biel's answer leaves no doubt that objective finality will play no part as a foundation for moral necessity and obligation. For he answers that a person should will in conformity with the divine will for this reason: simply "because it is *conformable* or because the divine will so *wills*." [11] This is rectitude for rectitude's sake. It is "ought" simply for the sake of "ought." The possibility of being obliged to will primarily to attain an end is herewith precluded.

This freedom of the will from any necessity imposed by the intellect is still maintained whenever the will does act for an end. For the will is free to choose the end of its actions. It is free to act for an end set by itself, in preference to one set by the intellect. And if the will can choose an end which is contrary to reason, it can also choose one which is beside reason: neither according to reason nor contrary to it. And it is able to do this because it is in the power of the will to have the use and enjoyment of created things or of its own self.[12]

Seeing that Biel puts such a premium on the will and its freedom,—in fact, making it the cornerstone of his psychology and morality—it may be well, before going on,

10 *Loc. cit.*
11 *Loc. cit.* (italics added).
12 *Ibid.*, d.41, q.1.

to glance briefly at how he goes about proving the freedom of the will.

He says, drawing on Ockham, that the fact that the will is free is evident "from experience." Therefore it cannot be demonstrated by anything more evident. For, first, man experiences within himself the fact that, regardless of whatever reason dictates should be willed, the will may will it or not. Secondly, any attempt to prove it otherwise than by experience, that is, by reasoning, either assumes something doubtful or less well known or equally unknown. Nevertheless it can be proved against those who deny it, by leading them to certain conclusions which all who have the use of reason judge to be false and inadmissible. For, if man would do or omit nothing through *liberum arbitrium*, then all human counsel would be in vain. Even a mule would merit reward or punishment for its acts. So also, divine precepts would be profitless to man if he did not come to his reward by freely observing them. It is also contrary to innumerable scriptural evidences. And, he concludes, many other absurd consequences could be mentioned.[13]

Command: act of will. The command, for Biel, is an act of the will. It is the "actual willing that something be done." [14] It may be either formally or virtually imperative, he explains, obviously following Ockham. It is formally imperative when it is an act of the will actually willing that something be done absolutely without any

13 *Ibid.*, d. 25, q. 1, M-O.
14 *Ibid.*, III, d. 36, q. 1, B.

conditions attached, or willing that something be accepted without rebelling against it. An example of this would be, if someone who intended to die for the defense of the faith would command his inferior powers to accept death without rebelling against it. This command is an imperative act. Or take the case of a man having much money who actually and efficaciously wills to give his money to the poor. Such an act of the will is actually a command to his exterior powers to give the money to the poor.[15]

A command, on the other hand, which is not formally imperative but only virtually or equivalently so, is to will something not absolutely but conditionally, namely, on the condition that an impediment be removed. For instance, if a pauper would will to give everything he owns for the sake of God—if he had it to give. Such a willing is not absolute. For he cannot reasonably will to give absolutely what he does not have to give, because of the impediment, namely, not having the wherewithal. Likewise, a virtual command would be to will to undergo death, if it were imminent, for the defense of the faith on account of the glory of God—but it is not now imminent. Such an act of the will is imperative, not formally, but only equivalently.[16]

Of course, such acts affect character since from them specifically different habits are formed. First, because they have specifically distinct objects. One act has the impediment for its object; the other, which is formally imperative, does not. Secondly, because, regardless of how much

15 *Loc. cit.*
16 *Loc. cit.*

the equivalently imperative act is increased, it will never incline to the formally imperative act. Thirdly, because these two acts can be separated. A person may have an equivalently imperative act or a habit with respect to an object, although he may never have a formally imperative act or habit in regard to the same object.[17]

As was noted above in regard to Ockham,[18] this position takes the election and the command to be one and the same act. The relation of the order of the means willed to the end is not considered as a formally distinct object requiring a formally distinct act. Hence, when considered as the command of a lawgiver, the *one* act of the will of the lawgiver is sufficient.

II

Law. Law (*lex*), Biel says, is so called either because of its derivation from the word ligate (*ligando*) or obligate (*obligando*), that is, to bind; or from the word lecture (*legendo*), that is, to dictate what is to be done. Such a law can be defined as "a true sign manifesting the dictate of right reason to a rational creature that he is obliged to do or not to do a certain thing." [19]

After saying that, if the sign were not manifested or made known, no one would be obliged [20] and that it must be of right reason in the lawgiver otherwise it would not be just,[21] Biel goes on to explain what is meant by the dic-

---

17 *Loc. cit.*
18 Cf. above, chap. 3.
19 *Ibid.*, d.37, q.1, a.1, A-B.
20 *Loc. cit.*
21 *Ibid.*, B.

tate of right reason. His use of this phrase seems, at first, inconsistent with what he has said with regard to the command: that it was an act of the will. But this is not true, for "dictate" here means not only an act of the reason but also an act of the will. The right reason of the lawgiver together with his will is the foundation for the obligation of the inferior. If, however, it should be asked which of these two, the intellect or the will, is ultimately the source of obligation, then it must be answered that it is the will. Even in regard to God, we are not obliged to will what we know that He wills. "We are obliged to will only what He wills that we will." [22]

Hence divine law is a "true sign of the divine right reason willing that the creature be obliged to do or not to do something for the attainment of eternal happiness." [23] Likewise natural law is a "naturally known sign of the divine right reason willing that the rational creature be obliged to do or not to do something for the attainment of his natural end which is human happiness, either individual, domestic, or political." [24] Human positive law is a "true sign of right reason, immediately constituted by human authority, willing to oblige the rational creature to do or not to do something for the attainment of a temporal or eternal end consonant with reason." [25]

In all these instances it is the *right reason* of the superior *willing* that the subject be obliged that is the essence of law and the source of obligation.[26]

[22] *Ibid.*, ante C.
[23] *Ibid.*, C.
[24] *Ibid.*, D.
[25] *Loc. cit.*
[26] This lack of preciseness of expression, whereby reason is said to will, may for Biel be due to the fact that he makes no real distinction between the in-

Obligation: from the will. Whatever necessity exists between the means and the end comes, then, from the will of the lawgiver commanding that the means be accomplished. For, explains Biel following Scotus,[27] in all mortal sin the will is disordered in regard to some means necessary for the end. But whence comes this necessity? "From the *divine will commanding* that this means be executed." [28]

So in regard to the Decalogue, Biel holds the same position as Scotus, whom he says he follows in this question.[29] Although the acts commanded by the first table—those formally concerned with the end—may be necessarily related to the end,[30] the acts commanded by the second table—those virtually concerned with the end—are not necessarily related to it. The only necessity they have in regard to the end comes from the fact that they are commanded by the divine will legislating. Contempt of parents, the killing of others, stealing, and adultery are not bad because they are of their objective essence opposed to the form and essence of man, and therefore necessarily against the attainment of his last end. They are bad because they are forbidden by the command of the divine will. If it were not for the fact of this prohibitive command, men could place all such acts and attain their end nevertheless.[31] "God could command that a man deceive another through a lie . . . and he would not sin." [32] "God could

---

tellect and the will. Suarez, *De leg.,* I, c. 12, n. 3, makes an interesting point of comparison. Cf. below, chap. 6.

27 Cf. above, chap. 2.

28 *Ibid.,* II, d. 35, q. 1, L (italics added).

29 *Ibid.,* III, d. 37, q. 1, a. 1, Q.

30 *Ibid.,* L.

31 *Ibid.,* M.

32 *Ibid.,* II, d. 38, q. 1, G.

remove the command in regard to lying and then the liar would not sin. . . . As long as the law stands, every pernicious, deliberate lie is a mortal sin." [33]

This is possible because the divine will is for Biel, as it was for Scotus and Ockham, the ultimate source and determinant of justice and injustice, of good and bad. If God wills something, "by that very fact whatever He has willed is just and good." The divine will alone, not the divine intellect or the divine essence, is the first rule of good and bad.[34]

With the necessity of means for the end deriving therefore from the command of the will of the lawgiver, it is not surprising to find Biel making a distinction between an indicative law and an imperative law.[35] An indicative law is one, expressed in the indicative mood, that indicates or signifies what should be done or should not be done. It does not, however, command that it be done or not be done. For instance, "Whoever is avaricious will not enter into Christ's kingdom" is an example of such a law.[36] An imperative law, on the other hand, is one, expressed in the imperative mood, that commands that a certain thing be done or not be done. Thus, "Thou shalt not steal" is an imperative law.[37] Now Biel has already said that obligation comes from the will of the legislator commanding. Hence it seems that only an imperative law could be said to oblige. And although he holds, of course, that the viola-

---

[33] *Loc. cit.* Cf. below, Bellarmine, chap. 12, for the opposite opinion.
[34] *Ibid.*, I, d.43, q.1, E.
[35] Cf. above, Scotus, chap. 2; Ockham, chap. 3; below, Suarez, chap. 6.
[36] *Ibid.*, II, d.35, q.1, D.
[37] *Ibid.*, ante E.

tion of an indicative, as well as of an imperative law, is a sin, yet he is willing to say that only a law which obliges is a true law.[38] If this seems to be an inconsistency, perhaps it can be partially explained by the fact that Biel was using two expressions, the full implication of which he did not seem to realize. The idea of a *lex indicativa,* which does not connote finality and obligation, is the product of Biel's theory of will. *Lex obligatoria,* on the other hand, is the product of another psychology, that in which the intellect representing order and necessity furnishes the foundation of obligation.

Purely penal law. A law that would not oblige in conscience to the doing or the not doing of the act specified, but only to the payment of the penalty: was this concept according to the mind of Biel?

At first sight it seems not. He quotes St. Thomas with approval, that human positive laws which are just oblige in conscience.[39] He also says, with St. Thomas, that the justness of a law comes from its end, author, and form.[40] Again, he agrees that laws oblige according to the mind of the legislator, in the sense that *epikeia* now and then has its place.[41]

It is only when Biel discusses the fact that all laws do not have the force of command and therefore do not oblige under mortal sin, that it becomes evident he holds that all laws do not oblige to the act specified.

[38] *Ibid.,* IV, d. 16, q. 3, H.
[39] *Ibid.,* J.
[40] *Ibid.,* K.
[41] *Ibid.,* L.

Biel says that not all statutes or laws have the force of command and therefore do not oblige under pain of mortal sin. Now, how can it be determined when a law obliges and when it does not? Biel gives three ways. The first is a corollary of his own psychology. A law has the force of command when it is evident that such is the *will* of the legislator.[42] If it is not evident what the will of the legislator is, then there is a second way. The *matter* of the law must be examined. If it is found to be something very necessary for the common good, then the law has the force of command. If, however, the matter is only useful, then the law does not have the force of command. For it is not to be presumed that the lawgiver would readily oblige under mortal sin without sufficient cause.[43] Thirdly, if it is not certain what the intention of the lawgiver is and it cannot be determined whether the matter is necessary or only useful, then the *words* of the law must be examined. If the words imply the threat of mortal sin (for instance: "we command," "we forbid"), then the law obliges under pain of mortal sin. If, however, the words do not imply such a threat (for instance: "we will," "we order," "we warn"), then the law does not oblige under pain of mortal sin.[44]

What is to be concluded from this passage? First, certainly, that if it is not the will of the lawgiver that a law should oblige under pain of mortal sin, then the law does

---

[42] *Ibid.,* M.

[43] *Loc. cit.* Biel certainly means that the matter of the law should be investigated in order that the intention and will of the lawgiver may be known. If he meant that the matter should be investigated because the matter of itself determines whether the law obliges, that would be inconsistent. For he has already said that it is the will of the lawgiver that determines this.

[44] *Loc. cit.*

not so oblige; and this because such a law lacks the force of command. Secondly, it seems it can be concluded that, if such a law lacks the force of command, it would not oblige at all, even under pain of venial sin. Otherwise there could be a law which did not have the force to command but which obliged under sin, even venial. Therefore it seems safe to conclude that it is according to Biel's mind that there could be a law which did not oblige in conscience under the pain of sin, mortal or venial, in regard to the act specified.

It should be noted that in this passage Biel is most surely confusing what in St. Thomas are two different questions: "whether human law imposes on men necessity in conscience," [45] and "whether a religious always sins mortally in transgressing those things that are in the rule." [46] Biel was not the first to confuse the two orders, religious and civil.[47] Nor was he to be the last.[48] Perhaps, too, this confusion is responsible for his failure to mention even the possibility of a law that obliged under the pain of only venial sin. It is also worth mentioning that his allowing the useful, as well as the necessary, to be the matter of law is later used as a basis of distinction between a pure penal law and a true moral law.[49]

Biel we find, then, is in the direct line of Henry of Ghent, Scotus, and Ockham. The main effect of his philosophy of will is to make law an act of the will. Whether a

[45] *Sum. theol.*, I–II, q. 16, a. 4.
[46] *Ibid.*, II–II, q. 186, a. 9. Cf. especially ad 2. Although Biel does not make this reference to Aquinas, it is evident that he had it in mind.
[47] Cf., for instance, above chap. 1.
[48] Cf. below, chap. 6.
[49] Cf. below, Castro, chap. 5; Suarez, chap. 6.

law obliges or not depends ultimately upon the will of the lawgiver. By his time the idea of a civil law that did not necessarily oblige in conscience directly in regard to what was specified must not have been too uncommon and its acceptance must not have been accompanied by too great difficulty.

CHAPTER V

ALPHONSE DE CASTRO

I

ALPHONSE DE CASTRO, O.F.M. (1495–1558) is important
as a well-known representative of a large segment of
thought of the early sixteenth century. He taught for
twenty years at the University of Salamanca and acted as
theological consultant to Cardinal Pacheo during the
early sessions of the Council of Trent.[1]

Castro followed the Franciscan tradition of Scotus.
Firmly convinced of the primacy of the will, he devoted
special attention to the consequences of such a philosophy
in regard to civil law. As a result, we have one of the first
works devoted entirely to this subject, entitled *De potestate legis poenalis* ("the force of penal law"). In it, as we
shall see, are put forth not only the arguments in favor of
civil penal law, but also the objections which adversaries
have raised against it. Castro's handling of these objections gives a further insight into the meaning of his position.

That Castro had no little influence on Suarez is shown

[1] For Castro's life and works, consult P. d'Alencon's article, "Castro," *Dictionnaire de théologie catholique*, II (1932), 1835–36; also Hurter, *Nomenclator*,
IV, 1184; Wadding, *Scriptores ordinis minorum* (Rome, 1650). He is not to be
confused with Paul de Castro (d. c. 1438) who wrote *Super codice* (Lyons, 1527).

by the references Suarez makes to him, usually for the purpose of substantiating an important point of doctrine.[2]

Will superior. Castro saw clearly that, for a foundation of law and therefore purely penal law, his position required a psychology that would free the will from any determination on the part of the intellect. Hence it is as basic with Castro as it was with Anselm, Henry of Ghent, Scotus, Ockham, and Biel that the will be clearly distinguished from nature. Nature operated by natural necessity, and this is the manner in which the intellect operated. But the will operated in an entirely different manner: it was free. The act of election in no way pertained to the intellect. It could be caused or necessitated by nothing outside itself.[3]

Command: of the will. This being so, the act of ordering (*ordinare*) and the act of commanding (*imperare*) could be acts only of the will.[4] Castro explicitly says that the act of command (as well as the acts of forbidding, permitting, and punishing) does not pertain to the intellect. It is properly an act of the will.[5] Hence the direction that

[2] Cf. below, Suarez, chap. 6. He also influenced Grotius. Cf. D. Stöckerl, "Castro," *Lexikon für Theologie und Kirche,* I (1930), 261.

[3] Alphonse de Castro, *La Fuerza de la Ley Penal* (Murcia, 1931), Bk. I, chap. 1, p. 16. The only available copy in the United States seems to be in the Harvard Law Library. Only Book I has thus far been printed.

[4] Suarez says: "Scotus is also cited for this opinion in 2, d.6, q.1 and d.38, q.1 *ad ult.* and *quodlib.* 17, inasmuch as he says in these places that it pertains to the will to order (*ordinare*) someone to do something, and in 3, d.36, q.1, ar. 2 he attributes the command (*imperare*) to the will. Castro fully defends the same opinion in libr. 2 *De lege poenali*, cap. 1" (*De legibus*, I, c.5, n.8).

[5] Castro, *op. cit.,* I, chap. 1, p. 14. As mentioned above (note 3), only Book I of Castro's *De potestate legis poenalis* is available. Hence, because his own

Castro's thought will take in regard to law is clearly indicated.

II

Law: act of the will. Proceeding immediately then to
his definition of law, Castro says it is "the right will of
him who rules in the name of the people, promulgated
orally or in writing, with the intention of obliging subjects to obey." [6] There are two important aspects of this
definition which need clarification: the meaning of right
will and the meaning of intention to oblige.

First, then, in regard to right will. Castro says he is using
the word "will" here, not to signify the tree power of the
soul itself, but rather to denote the acts of this power.
Hence this includes the acts "to will" and "to will not"
which in the will of the vicegerent of the people have the
force of law.[7]

Now, because election and ordering, as well as commanding, pertain to the will alone, the judgment of the
intellect itself cannot be a law. Just because a legislator
judges something should be done does not mean that a
law has been passed. Only when he *wills* that what is just
be done by the subjects is there a law. For "what pleases
the prince has the force of law." [8] This act of willing, then,

further development of these points of his psychology is not at hand, the
present treatment of his philosophy of intellect and will must necessarily be
brief and therefore somewhat unsatisfactory.

[6] *Ibid.*, p. 12.

[7] *Ibid.*, p. 13.

[8] *Ibid.*, chap. 2, p. 46; cf. *ibid.*, chap. 1, p. 13. Because Castro held this position
he rejects Cicero's definition of law, saying: "Cicero in the first book of the
De legibus in defining law says: 'Law is the *ratio summa* innate in nature
which commands those things that are to be done and forbids the contrary.'

is the act by which the lawgiver elects to establish a law
and it is from this very act that law (*lex*) gets its name.[9] It
is this act of the will that is the command by which the lawgiver forbids and permits.[10] In fact, because the election
which constitutes law is an act of the will, it is an error to
say that law is an act of prudence, as some have done.[11]
To be sure, prudence is necessary in the legislator in order
that he may know in regard to what he should legislate.
But it does not follow from this that law is an act of prudence. If this were so, it would have to be said that all
other virtues, which we call moral, would have to be called
prudence because none of them is capable of its own
proper act without the guidance of prudence.[12]

For these reasons, then, Castro defines law as a right
will. But whence is it right? Whence comes the rectitude
of the will? Is it from within the will: is it rectitude for its
own sake? Or is it from something outside the will, something that implies a relation to an end? Earlier authors
had a tendency to find the basis for rectitude of the will
within the will itself: "rectitude for the sake of rectitude."
But in later authors, such as Castro and Suarez and others,
there is manifested an inclination to explain the rectitude
of the will by a relation to something outside the will.
Thus Castro says that the rectitude of the will comes
"from a conformity with right reason or with pru-

Which definition, although it so satisfied Cicero that he often repeats it in
the same book, doubly errs in my judgment. First because what he says is
false and [secondly] it contains a contradiction" (*ibid.*, p. 45).

9 *Ibid.*, chap. 1, p. 14.
10 *Loc. cit.*
11 *Ibid.*, p. 16. Cf., for instance, St. Thomas, *Sum. theol.*, II–II, q. 47, a. 8.
12 *Loc. cit.*

dence." [13] This is to say that the will is right only if it conforms to the judgment of the intellect. Now, if it is of the
essence of law that it be just and right, so that there is no
law at all unless it be so,[14] and if its justness and rightness
come ultimately from a relation to the intellect, the question may well be raised: Is the essence of law ultimately of
the will or of the intellect? Is it possible to discuss the essence of law completely without discussing the act of the intellect—not simply as a *conditio sine qua non,* but as a true
cause? This difficulty becomes more apparent in Suarez.

Secondly, in regard to the lawgiver's intention to oblige.
This intention, Castro says, is not simply any intention the
lawgiver may have in regard to his subjects. It must be the
unique intention whereby he wills to oblige the subjects
to what the law decrees.[15] Thus, if the legislator would
counsel his subjects, that certainly would manifest his will
in regard to the matter which he counsels. It would not,
however, be a law because by it they would not be obliged
to do or not to do anything.[16] This is true because law has
the force of obliging and necessitating.[17]

Obligation: from the will. Here Castro has reached the
crucial point of necessity or obligation. What is its foundation? Is it the objective relation of means to end, or is it the
act of the will itself? Castro's metaphysics of will makes
only the latter answer possible. Necessity as well as motion

[13] *Loc. cit.*
[14] *Ibid.,* p. 17.
[15] *Ibid.,* p. 43.
[16] *Ibid.*
[17] *Ibid.,* p. 44.

can come "only from the will." It comes "from the command itself." [18]

Necessity here is to be taken, of course, as moral or conditioned necessity. An act is necessary on the condition that without it an end cannot be attained. But the meaning of such a necessity is immediately weakened by its being explained as that which is ordinarily called "useful." For this reason Castro believes that St. Thomas saves Isidore from being superfluous by establishing the distinction between the necessary, as that which refers to the removal of evil, and the useful, as that which pertains to the pursuit of good.[19] Castro does not go on to say, granting that St. Thomas kept Isidore's distinction and gave meaning to it, for St. Thomas the promotion of the good was also necessary, in the strictest possible sense. It is to be noted here, too, that the distinction between necessary and useful later serves as a basis for distinguishing between moral and penal law.[20]

Before coming to grips with the question of whether the lawgiver can enact a law that would not oblige under pain of sin, Castro first takes up the question of whether human authority, ecclesiastical or secular, can issue laws that do oblige at all.[21]

This question had been pointed up by the Lutherans and other heretics who claimed that no human law, not even ecclesiastical, could oblige men in conscience if it enjoined anything not contained explicitly in the divine

[18] *Loc. cit.*
[19] *Ibid.*, p. 23. Cf. *Sum. theol.*, I–II, q.95, a.3.
[20] Cf. below, Suarez, chap. 6.
[21] *Ibid.*, chap. 4, p. 92.

law. For them all human law had no moral content, strictly speaking.[22] John Gerson, Chancellor of the University of Paris a hundred years earlier, had given support to this position. For he said that only God could pass laws whose transgression would be such an offense that it would deserve eternal punishment. If a human law did oblige under pain of mortal sin, it would be because it was mixed with a divine law.[23] It was this position of Gerson that Luther adduced in support of his own, in which he held that no human law could oblige men in conscience.[24]

Castro says that Gerson's basic error is to be found in his failure to distinguish between human laws that are enacted on the authority of men alone and human laws that are enacted on God's authority, delegated to ecclesiastical prelates and civil rulers.[25] These latter laws, then, founded on the authority of God, can oblige in conscience.

When does the civil law oblige under the pain of mortal sin? When the matter is so necessary for the commonwealth that its omission is deserving of eternal punishment.[26] Because many matters contained in civil law are not of this nature, the law may oblige only under pain of venial sin.[27] At this mention of an objective norm for determining the gravity of obligation, namely, the matter of law, the question immediately arises: Has Castro overlooked the subjective norm, the will of the legislator? The answer follows immediately. He says that a law obliges

[22] *Ibid.*, p. 93.
[23] *Loc. cit.;* cf. *ibid.*, p. 136.
[24] *Ibid.*, p. 94. Cf. below, Bellarmine, chap. 12.
[25] *Ibid.*, p. 137; cf. *ibid.*, p. 140.
[26] *Ibid.*, chap. 5, p. 161.
[27] *Ibid.*, p. 164.

under pain of mortal or venial sin according to the will of the lawgiver which can be determined by the words of the law. Why is this so? Because all obligation depends on the will of the lawgiver. If he wishes to oblige under pain of mortal or venial sin, that depends solely on his intention.[28]

Hence Castro in the passage mentioned above says it is the matter and the will of the lawgiver which determine the gravity of obligation. Is this a contradiction? Not for Castro—so it seems—because the will always has to be rectified by conformity to right reason, and right reason would take account of the gravity of the matter. This, however, still leaves us with the difficulty mentioned above. If right reason in its relation to objective reality enters into the very essence of law and obligation, can law and obligation be defined as essentially acts of the will?

Purely penal law. Having said, against Gerson and Luther and others, that human laws can oblige under pain of sin on account of authority given by God, Castro is now ready to show that there may be human laws which do not oblige in conscience at all in regard to the acts specified by the law.

There can be three types of laws: those which oblige in conscience, but with no penalty attached, a moral law pure and simple; [29] those which oblige in conscience with a penalty attached, a mixed penal law; [30] and those which do not oblige in conscience, but only impose a penalty, a purely penal law.[31] Hence there are really two kinds of

[28] *Ibid.,* p. 172.
[29] *Ibid.,* chap. 8, p. 279.
[30] *Ibid.,* chap. 9, pp. 305 f.
[31] *Ibid.,* pp. 304 f.

penal law: one that is a mixed penal law and one that is a purely penal law.

Castro says that this distinction of penal law was held by Henry of Ghent, who, even though he did not use the same words, by his examples showed he had the same idea.[32] This distinction, however, was not regarded with favor in all quarters. For instance, Sylvester ("with no urbanity or civility," Castro says) ridicules it, saying it is purely verbal and puerile. Castro's purpose, then, is to show that this distinction is anything but "verbal" and "puerile," [33] and that there is a real distinction between a purely penal law and a mixed penal law. For a purely penal law does not command or oblige, whereas a mixed penal law does.[34]

Why, then, does a purely penal law not command and oblige in conscience? Because it does not contain any word which indicates that it was the will of the lawgiver that it so oblige.[35] For instance, it does not contain such words as "I command," "I forbid," "you are obliged," "it is necessary," "I ordain in virtue of holy obedience," which words indicate that the lawgiver wills to oblige in conscience.[36] In a word, a purely penal law does not oblige in conscience because there is in the law no word manifesting such an obligation.[37]

But how can the lawgiver impose a penalty if no fault

[32] *Ibid.*, p. 304. Here Castro quotes the entire passage mentioned above, chap. 1, note 37.

[33] *Loc. cit.* The reference here is to Sylvester Prierias, O.P. (1460–1523), also called Mozolini or Mazzolini. His best known work is his *Summa Sylvestrina* (Rome, 1516; Lyons, 1594).

[34] *Ibid.*, pp. 321 f.

[35] *Ibid.*, p. 322.

[36] *Ibid.*, p. 323.

[37] *Ibid.*, p. 326.

has preceded it? Does not *poena* necessarily presuppose *culpa?* This is a difficulty which Castro must face and solve. If the penalty necessarily depends on the commission of a fault, how can there be a law which imposes a penalty but does not impose an obligation the violation of which would be a fault?

Castro's answer in general is that there can be a penalty without a preceding *culpa,* though there cannot be a penalty without a *causa.* "Frequently punishment is imposed on someone without his fault, although it is never imposed upon someone without a cause." [38] Hence the fact that a purely penal law imposes a penalty does not mean, says Castro, that there must have been a preceding fault and therefore an obligation in conscience in regard to the act specified by the law.[39]

Sylvester, who seems to have brought the sharpest attack to bear against the concept of purely penal law, had said that if a lawgiver enacted a law it was for the purpose of having something done or omitted. And if this were the case, he could not help but oblige in conscience.[40]

Castro meets this attack, first, by denying outright that when the legislator intends that something be done or not be done he always thereby wills that the subjects be obliged to act accordingly. Frequently, he says, it happens that the one having authority wills something to be done and so manifests his will, yet he does not will to oblige. This is true even with God. God manifests His will to us

[38] *Ibid.,* p. 327. Castro may here be under the influence of Henry of Ghent; cf. above, chap. 1, note 42.
[39] *Ibid.,* p. 328.
[40] *Ibid.,* p. 329.

through His counsels, but He does not thereby intend to oblige us to do what He counsels. The same is true in regard to the counsels of men.[41]

Secondly, Castro argues against Sylvester's difficulty, saying that, just as a legislator shows what he wills to be done by a law which obliges in conscience, so also without any obligation in conscience and solely by the fear of punishment he can induce his subjects to do or not to do that on account of which the punishment is imposed.[42]

Again, Castro says, there is the example of religious orders, in which the statutes do not oblige in conscience. Hence it does not follow that a legislator who intends something to be done, for that reason intends to oblige in regard to that thing.[43] If it is objected that this is the case in religious orders, because it is stated in the statutes that they do not oblige in conscience, as in the statutes of the Franciscans and the Dominicans, then Castro answers that this fact only shows the possibility of having a law in which the legislator does not intend to oblige his subjects in conscience.[44]

It is false therefore, Castro says, that the legislator in every penal law always intends that the thing be done or omitted on account of which the penalty is imposed. Nor does it follow from this that such a purely penal law is tyrannical. Because, although there would be no fault preceding, it is sufficient that a cause precede, so that it is on

[41] *Ibid.*, pp. 334 f.
[42] *Ibid.*, p. 335.
[43] *Loc. cit.* Attention must again be called to the tendency ever present in some authors to treat the problem of purely penal civil law as if it were the same as the problem of purely penal religious law.
[44] *Ibid.*, pp. 335 f.; cf. *ibid.*, p. 337.

account of it that the penalty is imposed. "For it often happens that someone, without any fault of his own, may lack certain qualifications necessary for the proper exercise of an office. And for this reason, although without his fault, this penalty is justly inflicted upon him, that he assume such an office or, having assumed it, that he be not able to fulfill it." [45]

What judgment should be passed on Castro's critique of the *culpa-poena* relation? Castro says there can be a penalty if there is a cause preceding it. What is such a cause? It is certainly not too clear from the example just given. In fact, in view of what he says below concerning the ultimate relation between a purely penal law and a mixed penal law, the *causa* which he says is sufficient for a penalty may, after all, turn out to be a *culpa*.

Against this concept of purely penal law stands the classic objection: If a purely penal law does not oblige in conscience, it is not a true law but only a counsel or something similar which does not oblige. [46]

Castro's answer to this difficulty is twofold and gives a new meaning and extension to the concept of obligation. He says, first, that if the penal law states a penalty to be imposed by a judge, then the law obliges the judge to impose such a punishment. If, on the other hand, the penal law states a penalty that is immediately effective upon violation, then the law obliges the violator to pay the penalty. [47] Secondly, he says that sometimes a fault is committed by doing or omitting that on account of which

45 *Ibid.*, p. 340.
46 *Ibid.*, pp. 340 f.
47 *Ibid.*, p. 341.

the penalty is imposed. In such cases, then, the obligation has been induced by another law, a moral law. In other words, a purely penal law may oblige in conscience, but it is in virtue of an obligation imposed by another law.[48]

Therefore it is possible, Castro concludes, for a purely penal law to oblige the judge to impose the penalty and the violator to sustain the penalty, but of itself it cannot oblige to the doing or the not doing of that on account of which the penalty was imposed. Because of a failure to realize this distinction, Castro says, Sylvester was deceived when he cited St. Thomas in support of his position, that all laws oblige in conscience. Castro says he is willing to concede, with St. Thomas, that human laws oblige in conscience, but they do not oblige beyond what was intended by the laws themselves. Purely penal laws intend only the penalty. Therefore, if of themselves they oblige in any way, it is to the payment of the penalty. Castro says: "Cajetan, who (as I believe) knew the mind of St. Thomas much better than Sylvester, favors this same opinion." [49]

It is of some importance, then, to see how Cajetan, according to Castro, interprets St. Thomas in favor of purely penal law. The passage of Cajetan referred to by Castro is concerned with the question, whether it is licit for a religious to beg. Cajetan says that someone begging out of a desire for a lazy life, from which indeed he is a pauper, commits no fraud against the neighbor. He sins only against himself by choosing a lazy and abject way of life without any reasonable cause. Hence there is no question

[48] *Ibid.*, p. 342.
[49] *Ibid.*, pp. 341 f. The reference to St. Thomas is to the *Sum. theol.*, I–II, q.96, a.4.

here of mortal sin. Then Cajetan goes on to say—and this
is the phrase which Castro believes supports his position
—that neither is there question of mortal sin on account
of the punishment imposed by civil law, which a beggar
may have to undergo. For such punishment does not cause
a fault, but "punishes a fault already presupposed which
in itself is not mortal." [50] Castro concludes from these
words of Cajetan that Cajetan holds that such a law does
not oblige under pain of sin. The reason Cajetan says this,
Castro explains, is "because it is a mere penal law, which
commands nothing but only imposes a penalty." [51]

What is this fault which Cajetan says is presupposed
before there can be punishment? Is Cajetan saying the
same thing as Sylvester: that there can be no law which
imposes a penalty unless that same law also obliges in conscience? Castro says, No. When, he says, Cajetan speaks of
a fault being presupposed, it is from another law, a moral
law.[52] If a penal law, which imposes a penalty, is mixed so
that it first commands something to be done or not to be
done and afterwards imposes a penalty, through the imposition of such a penalty it indicates that what is legislated by such a law obliges under pain of mortal sin. If, on
the other hand, the law is purely penal, it indicates a prior
moral law, divine or human, obliging under pain of mortal sin if that on account of which the penalty was imposed
is done or omitted.[53] This, concludes Castro, is what Cajetan meant when he spoke of a presupposed fault. It is pre-

[50] *Ibid.*, p. 346.
[51] *Ibid.*, p. 347.
[52] *Loc. cit.*
[53] *Ibid.*, pp. 349 f.

supposed from another law, not from this purely penal law which only imposes the penalty.[54]

We can only wonder why Castro does not discuss the possibility that Cajetan could have meant that no law can impose a punishment unless for a fault committed by failure to do what the law itself commands and obliges. To interpret this text of Cajetan as Castro has done seems to indicate that he was grasping for some evidence which would show that the theory of purely penal law was not against the principles of St. Thomas. Sylvester had said that it was against these principles. Now Cajetan, at least according to Castro, says it was not. But further reading of Cajetan makes it extremely difficult to agree with Castro's interpretation of him.[55]

With this tendency in Castro to say that any obligation in purely penal law must come from another moral or mixed law, what would Castro say in regard to certain things which today are said by some to be the matter of purely penal law and therefore not to oblige in conscience?

For instance, Castro discusses the case of the time in 1539 when the amount of rainfall had been very small. In consequence the corn, wheat, and barley crop was alarmingly light. Therefore the king, Charles, to protect the poor set a ceiling price on corn, wheat, and barley. If anyone bought or sold beyond this price he was fined.[56] Now the question arises: Did such a law oblige in conscience? Some said that, because the law was penal, it did not oblige in conscience. Hence violators were not bound to restitu-

[54] *Ibid.*, p. 350.
[55] Cf. below, Cajetan, chap. 9.
[56] *Ibid.*, chap. 12, pp. 432 f.

tion.[57] Castro, however, disagrees with this opinion. He holds that, because of the words used, there is indicated a command which obliges. This is from another law, the divine law, which forbids stealing. Therefore this law is a mixed law and obliges in conscience. Violators are consequently obliged to restitution.[58]

Would Castro interpret all so-called purely penal laws in this fashion, as mixed penal laws? Would he always find the matter of a purely penal law also the matter of another moral law? If so, then all purely penal laws would ultimately oblige in conscience.[59] The only alternative is to say that in some laws the matter is indifferent, that it has no actual relation to the common good. But in that event why should it be the matter of a law at all, since a law is just only if its matter is necessary for the common good? Not being of a mind preoccupied with the objective relation of the matter of law to the common good, Castro seems not to have bothered asking himself these questions.

In sum, Castro says a purely penal law, as such, can never of itself oblige to that on account of which the penalty is imposed. If it did, then there could be a purely penal law, without any human or divine moral law preceding it, which commanded and obliged in regard to that on account of which the penalty is imposed. But this, he says, is never the case. If it ever seems so, it only indicates that the lawgiver has not manifested his intention clearly.[60]

The obligation, then, imposed by a mixed penal law

[57] *Ibid.*, p. 433.
[58] *Ibid.*, pp. 433 f.; cf. *ibid.*, pp. 442 f.
[59] This seems to be the reason why Navarrus wonders whether all penal laws are not mixed laws. Cf. *Consiliorum sive responsorum pars secunda, de lege poenali* (Cremona, 1591), p. 825.
[60] *Ibid.*, chap. 9, p. 351.

comes from no other source than the intention and will of
the lawgiver by which he wills to oblige. Just as the goodness or badness of the exterior act comes from the goodness
or badness of the interior act by which it is commanded, so
the obligation of law depends upon the interior act of the
will of the one willing to oblige by his law. Thus, as mentioned, the statutes of religious orders do not oblige in
conscience because their legislators did not so intend.
Hence varying degrees of obligation of laws depend directly on the varying intentions of the lawgiver. If one law
obliges more than another, it is simply because the lawgiver so wills.[61] This intention and will can be determined
by the words of the law. Depending upon the words used,
the will of the lawgiver can be ascertained: whether he
intends to oblige under pain of mortal or of venial sin.[62]

Castro is a man who consistently applied his psychology
of will to his philosophy of law. Being necessitated by
nothing outside itself causally, but only conditionally, the
will and the will alone elected, directed, and commanded.
Hence the command of law, and therefore the essence of
law, was of the will. Obligation and the varying degrees of
it have the will as their source. When confronted with
the objection that, if a purely penal law does not oblige,
then it is no law at all, he is willing to say that it is ultimately a law because it obliges in virtue of another law
which does oblige.

This is the philosophical climate in which Suarez found
himself.

61 *Ibid.*, chap. 12, p. 401.
62 *Ibid.*, pp. 401, 402 f.

CHAPTER VI

FRANCIS SUAREZ

I

FRANCIS SUAREZ, S.J. (1548–1617), was a man of vast erudition, and his knowledge of the history of philosophy was immense. He started his long teaching career at Segovia in 1571. He taught at the Roman College from 1580 to 1585, at Alcala from 1585 to 1593, at Salamanca from 1593 to 1597, and at Coimbra from 1597, with interruptions, until 1615. That Suarez was predominantly under the influence of Scotus, and Ockham too, is shown by the fact that he holds with him on such key theses as the direct intellectual knowledge of material things, the individuation of sensible things independently of their matter, the real identity of essence and existence, the identity of matter and form considered in themselves, and, as we shall see, the primacy of the will. He is justly famous for his great treatise *De legibus,* which is unquestionably one of the most thorough treatments of the relation between the concept of law and the philosophy of intellect and will ever written. No effort is spared by Suarez in examining every aspect of both terms of this relation.[1]

[1] For Suarez' life and works in general, consult R. de Scorraille, S.J., *François Suarez de la Compagnie de Jesus* (Paris: Lethielleux, 1912). His doctrine is well treated in Leon Mahieu, *François Suarez, sa philosophie et les rapports qu'elle a avec sa théologie* (Paris: Desclée, 1921). Cf. also K. Werner, *F. Suarez und die Scholastik der letzten Jahrhunderte* (2nd ed., Ratisbonne, 1889).

Will superior. Why did Suarez hold that the will was the more important faculty? The answer to this question entails certain historical difficulties if one takes into account all the writings of Suarez. For in his earlier works he is inclined to be much more "intellectualistic" than he was afterward.[2] Hence it is only by considering his later works that we can hope to arrive at what was his most mature and final thought on this subject. It is here that we find him attributing to the will acts which are ordinarily (especially by St. Thomas) reserved for the intellect, and freeing the will from any necessity imposed by the intellect, thus denying the intellect a causal part in the action of the will.

Thus, to be a rule or measure pertains to the will since, as St. Thomas says, it is the divine will which is the first rule according to which human acts should be measured. The will of the human superior, then, is a secondary rule participating in the first.[3] It is the will also which enlightens, as St. Anselm had said.[4] Finally, "to order belongs to the will, as Scotus rightly taught. For it is the will which ordains [*ordinat*] means to the end, since the will itself intends the end and chooses the means on account of

[2] Thus in the *De anima*, V, c.5, n.2 (written during the first years of his teaching, 1571 and 1580), he says, "The intellect is the more perfect power." At the time of his death in 1617 Suarez was in the process of revising this work, but had gotten only as far as the first twelve chapters. Cf. R. Brouillard, "Suarez," *Dictionnaire de théologie catholique*, XIV (1941), 2641; also R. de Scorraille, S.J., *op. cit.*, II, 415. In the *De voluntario et involuntario* (first taught in Rome, 1581) Suarez holds that the *imperium* is of the intellect—which he later denied in the *De legibus;* cf. below, note 19.

[3] Suarez, *Tractatus de legibus ac Deo legislatore*, III, c.5, n.11. Why Suarez did not take into account what St. Thomas says in *Sum. theol.*, I–II, q.93, a.1 ad 2, can only be conjectured. There Aquinas says that it is the divine intellect which is the measure of all things.

[4] *Ibid.*, n.12.

the end and so determines that they be accomplished." [5]

If this appears to conflict with other statements of Suarez in which he says that it pertains to the intellect to enlighten, direct, and regulate and to the will only to move,[6] then the only conclusion that can be drawn is either that he later changed his position, or that he was willing to attribute the same acts to different faculties, thereby breaking down the specification of powers by formally distinct acts. Whatever should be said on this point, one thing is clear: Suarez, in giving the will the power of regulating, enlightening, and ordering, is making the will independent of the intellect and of any necessity deriving therefrom.

This desire to free the will from necessity imposed by the intellect becomes more apparent in Suarez' explanation of the interaction of intellect and will in the act of election.

Suarez is not at all satisfied with the stand taken by some followers of St. Thomas: that preceding the election there must be an act of the intellect determining the will, for otherwise the will would act without an object and without reason.[7] Such a position, especially as put forward by Medina and Bellarmine, is contradictory, Suarez says, to that held by Henry of Ghent and Scotus, and the Scotists generally—and with good reason. For such a position destroys liberty. Why? Because once the act of the intellect is placed, the will has no choice. The intellect necessitates it to "choose" this way rather than that.[8]

[5] *Ibid.*, n. 13. Cf. above, chap. 2, in regard to Scotus.
[6] *Metaphysicarum disputationum tomi duo,* XIX, c.6, n.7.
[7] *Loc. cit.*
[8] *Ibid.*, n.2.

How explain, then, the act of election? The only judgment on the part of the intellect that is necessary in regard to the goodness or badness of the act is the act's usefulness or fitness. After that no other judgment is necessary or possible. Any judgment that would determine the will to action (for instance, "This must be done") would by that very fact destroy liberty.[9] In fact, regardless of what judgment the intellect makes concerning the value of various means, the will is free to choose whichever means it wills, without any accompanying determining judgment.[10]

True, the indifference of the judgment is the root of liberty. This does not mean, however, that the intellect is formally free. It means only that it is objectively indifferent, that is, it so proposes indifferent objects that the will is not moved by necessity.[11] What should be said, therefore, is that *liberum arbitrium* pertains to the intellect radically and to the will formally. Nor is this against Henry of Ghent and Scotus, who deny that reason is the root of liberty and say it is only a necessary condition. It is only "a matter of words." For, since cognition is merely a necessary condition before willing, they wish to call the mode of cognition a necessary condition to the mode of volition which consists in liberty.[12]

For Suarez, the complete self-determination of the will and its independence from necessity is shown in his answer to the objection that, if the judgment of the intellect is undetermined how can the election of the will be determined. Suarez answers that the judgment cannot be called

9 *Ibid.*, n. 10.
10 *Ibid.*, n. 11.
11 *Ibid.*, c. 4, n. 4.
12 *Ibid.*, c. 5, n. 21.

undetermined when it is through it that the nature of an object as well as its fitness (*convenientia*) is judged. But what it can be called is either a multiple judgment when it judges the nature of many objects, or a determined judgment about an indifferent object, that is, "one not having a necessary connection with the will, though it may have some goodness and fitness." Such a determination of judgment, although it does not suffice to impose necessity on the will, suffices for the will through its own liberty to determine and follow this judgment.[13]

We must note here that Suarez, like Scotus, in rejecting the possibility of physical necessity being placed upon the will by the intellect, has by the same stroke removed the possibility of moral necessity and obligation being imposed upon the will by the intellect. To speak of the *convenientia* of an act is to speak of its relation to a rule or end, that is, its goodness or badness. But, if the will is not morally necessitated and obliged to place or avoid good or bad acts because the intellect has presented them as such, then by what can the will be obliged? The only thing left is the will itself, and the foundation of obligation becomes subjective.

But was not the explanation of the mutual causality of the intellect and will (as given, for instance, by St. Thomas) sufficient to explain the act of election—the will determining itself efficiently, and the intellect determining the will in regard to the end? Suarez says this explanation is not satisfactory. First, because "it is not based on any good reason." Secondly, it is not necessary. Finally, the mind

[13] *Ibid.,* c.6, n.12.

cannot conceive this mutual priority and motion between these two acts. In fact, it is impossible. For in every vital act a sufficient application of the object cannot effectively come from the act to which it is ordered. But a judgment of reason is required for the act of the will applying the object. Therefore it is impossible that the judgment of reason necessary for the act of the will come from the same act.[14] And as in vital acts, so in things of nature. It is impossible for an agent to act before it is presented with the patient. But the application of the patient before the act cannot be accomplished by the act itself which follows upon the application of the patient. Hence it is impossible that the application of the patient and the act of the agent upon the patient be one and the same act.[15]

Not only is Suarez, then, at pains to keep the will free in regard to exercise, but also in regard to specification. For, even though the will is confronted with a right practical judgment, it is not necessitated by it. The intellect can still consider other objects, judging them to be desirable, and the will is free to choose them.[16]

Again we have here an example of Suarez rejecting at one and the same time any physical as well as moral necessity imposed upon the intellect by the will. For, in not allowing the intellect to determine the will physically he also does not allow it to necessitate the will morally. In the passage considered above Suarez says that the will is free

---

[14] *Ibid.*, n. 5.

[15] *Loc. cit.* It is interesting to note the difference between this passage and the one in the *De anima* (V, c. 7, n. 6), written some twenty years earlier, in which Suarez says with St. Thomas that the intellect can move the will *finaliter*, and the will can move the intellect *effective*.

[16] *De angelis*, VII, c. 6, n. 15.

not to follow a right practical judgment. This undoubtedly is true as far as physical freedom is concerned, but it is not true in regard to moral freedom. The will is morally necessitated to follow a right practical judgment. Suarez' failure to make this distinction here, had its result later in his concept of obligation.

Command: act of the will. In regard to the act of command Suarez correctly understood St. Thomas, that there must be an act of the intellect *after* the election, commanding the executive powers to carry out what has been elected.[17] But in a capital passage Suarez rejects such an act of the intellect, saying that, as far as the individual himself is concerned, it is not required and in fact "it is not even possible." For the executive power is blind and cannot perceive the force of the command. Besides, it does not pertain to the intellect to apply a power to action. The intellect simply proposes an object to the will. Therefore it belongs to the will to apply other powers to action.[18]

Hence there is no command of the intellect after the election. The election is the principle of motion as well as of direction of the executive powers. Therefore, since such an act both elects and directs, it can also be called a command. If so, then command is of the will.[19]

17 *De leg.,* I, c.4, n.10.
18 *Ibid.,* n.11.
19 As mentioned above (note 2), Suarez' philosophy of intellect and will underwent a change. In the *De voluntario et involuntario* (IX, c.3, n.4) he held that first there was a practical judgment before the election. Then immediately after the election there was another judgment, a practically practical judgment, which directed the execution of the act. Suarez seems to be willing to call this last judgment the *imperium,* coming as it does after the act of the will (*De vol. et invol.,* IX, c.3, n.7).

Evidently Suarez does not believe there is question here of two distinct objects requiring two distinct acts, as St. Thomas did. For Suarez the electing to do a certain act is the same as the directing of its execution. For St. Thomas there were two formally distinct objects and two formally distinct acts involved here. The object of one act is to elect to act or not to act. The object of the other act, given the election to act, is to order and direct the accomplishment of what has just been elected. And because for St. Thomas direction or order is an act which only the intellect is capable of, it is attributed to the intellect and called command to distinguish it from the election, which is of the will. But for Suarez the will could assume the ordering and directing. Hence, for him, either you must say that there is no command of the intellect or that the command, as he understands it, is of the will.

With command, then, estabished as synonymous with election and therefore of the will, Suarez' philosophy of intellect and will gives the clue regarding what his concept

---

In comparing this passage with the others cited above from the *De legibus,* it should be kept in mind that the *De voluntario* was taught as a course in Rome beginning October 20, 1581. It was taken down by Suarez' students and published posthumously in 1628 without any revision by Suarez. The *De legibus,* on the other hand, was written by Suarez some twenty years later (between 1601 and 1603). It was prepared by Suarez himself for the press and published in 1612. Cf. R. de Scorraille, *op. cit.,* I, 174; II, 151. Whether Suarez' philosophy of intellect and will was affected by the controversy *De auxiliis,* which was raging at the very time he was writing the *De legibus,* would make an interesting study.

Curiously enough, in a recently published work which attempts to show that Suarez held the same position as St. Thomas in regard to the command being an act of the intellect, the references are not to the *De legibus,* but to the *De voluntario.* Cf. P. Jesus Muños, S.J., "Escencia del Libre Albedrio y Proceso del Acto Libre según F. Romeo, O.P., Sto. Tomas y F. Suarez, S.J.," *Miscelanea Comillas,* IX (Santander: Universidad Pontifica Comillas, 1948), 349–504.

of law will be, a thing of the will. With the will under no necessity to accept what is proposed by the intellect, the foundation of obligation is already indicated, the will itself.

II

Law: act of the will. Since, for Suarez, there is no act after the election, then law must be the act of election itself. Therefore it is of the will. Consistent with this, we find Suarez defining law as, "the act of a just and right will by which the superior wills to oblige the inferior to do this or that." [20] This is perhaps the clearest definition of law in Suarez. He also says, more generally, that law is "a common precept, just and permanent, sufficiently promulgated." [21] Confronted with St. Thomas' definition of law, namely, "Law is an ordination of reason for the common good by him who has the care of the community —promulgated," Suarez explains that the word "reason" does not necessarily mean the intellect in opposition to the will. It can refer to the will as well as to the intellect. An act of the will can be said to be of reason either because the will itself is a rational potency or because it ought to be directed by right reason, especially in enacting a law.[22]

---

[20] *De leg.*, I, c.5, n.24. The importance of the will in Suarez' theory of law is discussed in E. Jombart, S.J., "La volontarisme de la loi d'après Suarez," *Nouvelle revue théologique*, LIX (1932), 34–44. See also J.-T. Delos, *La société internationale et les principes du droit public* (Paris: Pedone, 1929), and its refutation by J. de Blic, "Le volontarisme juridique chez Suarez," *Revue de philosophie*, X (New Series, 1930), 213–30.

[21] *Ibid.*, c.12, n.4.

[22] *Ibid.*, n.3. It is difficult to avoid the conclusion that Suarez' handling of this passage in St. Thomas (*Sum. theol.*, I–II, q.90, a.1) is a piece of forced exegesis. That by "reason" Aquinas meant "intellect" as *opposed* to "will" is

Hence, presupposing what was established above, that in the individual there is no act of the intellect after the election, Suarez says that for law the only act necessary in the lawgiver after the act of the will is the manifestation of his will to oblige his subjects.[23] The only incidental act of the intellect would be that involved in speaking to the subjects.[24]

Suarez knows, of course, that he is taking a position contrary to the one held by St. Thomas, Cajetan, and Soto: that law is an act of the intellect.[25] But, Suarez points out, they are not even in agreement among themselves about which act of the intellect law is. Some say it is the judgment which precedes the election; others say it is the command which follows the election.[26]

But, argues Suarez, law cannot be the judgment which precedes the election, because this judgment does not have the power of obliging or of moving morally. Nor does it differ from the judgment of counsel, because the one counseling has a similar judgment about what should be done.[27] Nor can law be the command of the intellect. For, if the command is not a speaking to the subjects, then it is nothing. But if it is a speaking to the subjects, then it is more of the nature of a sign than of a law. And a sign pre-

---

clearly shown by the third objection, wherein it is argued that law is an act of the will. This, in his response (ad 3), St. Thomas emphatically denies, saying that law must be an act of reason. Reason, therefore, is here opposed by St. Thomas to the will. It is used as synonymous with intellect.

23 *Ibid.*, c.4, n.12.

24 *Ibid.*, n.14.

25 *Ibid.*, c.5, n.1.

26 *Ibid.*, n.5.

27 *Loc. cit.* Suarez here seems to have overlooked the fact that later he himself was going to give the distinction between this judgment and counsel, namely, the judgment is by one in authority (*ibid.*, c.12, n.4).

supposes that of which it is a sign, namely, a law.[28] Hence law cannot be an act of the intellect: it can be neither the judgment immediately preceding the election nor the command which follows it.

Suarez then, because of these difficulties in the intellectualistic position, feels constrained to turn to the doctrine of Henry of Ghent, Biel, Ockham, Bonaventure, Scotus, and Castro.[29] He does this not only because of the negative reason that there can be no act of the intellect after the election which could be law, but also because of the more positive reason that the various properties of law more properly belong to the will than to the intellect. Thus it is a property of law to be a rule and a measure. But to be a rule and a measure, as we have seen, pertains to the will. Therefore law is of the will.[30]

Then, too, a property of law is to enlighten and direct. But to enlighten and direct are also acts of the will of the legislator. On this point Suarez warns that sometimes when law is defined as of reason it does not refer to law in the legislator but in the subject, as for instance, when it is said that law is right reason constituted by nature.[31]

Finally, law orders means to the end and, since ordering is most properly an act of the will, as Scotus said, law is consequently an act of the will. For it is the will which intends the end and chooses the means because of the end.[32]

Law, then, is for Suarez an act of the will, first, because

28 *Ibid.*, c.5, n.6.
29 *Ibid.*, n.8.
30 *Ibid.*, n.11.
31 *Ibid.*, n.12.
32 *Ibid.*, n.13.

there is no act besides the election which could be law, and secondly, because the properties of law (to regulate, measure, enlighten, direct, and order) pertain to the will. Suarez can take this position since he is willing to blur the clear and sharp distinction between the intellect and will as powers that are distinct because their acts are distinct, and this because they have formally distinct objects. Further, his willingness to admit that the natural law may be a thing of reason whereas all other law is of the will, jeopardizes the possibility of a generic definition of law that can be verified in all its species. Otherwise law becomes equivocal and is no longer analogous.

Obligation: from the will. For Suarez, obligation is the principal intrinsic effect of law.[33] In fact, there could not be a law which did not induce some obligation, some necessity of acting or not acting.[34] But what is the source of this necessity? Is it the objective relation of means to end as presented by the intellect? From what we have already seen of Suarez' insistence on keeping the will free from any necessity, physical or moral, imposed by the intellect, such an objective foundation is ruled out.

Only the will, then, can be the source of necessity and obligation, if Suarez is to be consistent with his philosophy of intellect and will. So Suarez declares that the intellect can only *show* the necessity of an act. It cannot confer it. Only the will can *confer* necessity.[35] Therefore the reason why law induces necessity and obligation is not

[33] *Ibid.,* c. 14, n. 1.
[34] *Ibid.,* n. 4.
[35] *Ibid.,* c. 5, n. 15.

that it ordains what is objectively necessary for an end, but
that it is the command of the efficacious will of the one in
power willing to oblige. An efficacious will always produces its effect. Hence it is for this reason and this alone
that a law induces obligation.[36]

Since it is the will to oblige that really makes a law preceptive, Suarez is not averse to admitting the distinction
already made by Scotus, Ockham, and Biel between an
indicative law and a preceptive law. The indicative law, expressed in the indicative mood, is in the intellect and only
expresses a judgment that indicates what should be done:
because no will to oblige is involved, it does not oblige.
The imperative or preceptive law however, expressed in
the imperative mood, is in the will; because it entails the
will to oblige, it obliges.[37]

If it should be asked whether the intention to make a
law and the intention to oblige the subjects are one and
the same act, the answer is, Yes; because the essential act
required in the will of the legislator for the making of a
law is the will to oblige the subject. This is the preceptive
will, without which obligation has no meaning. Hence
the will to make a law is none other than the will to inti-
mate to the subject the intention to oblige him. Therefore
the will to make a law includes the will to oblige the subject, and vice versa.[38] In other words, in the act of election
is contained the intention both of making the law and of
obliging the subjects.[39]

[36] *Ibid.,* c. 14, n. 4.
[37] *De bonitate et malitia humanorum actuum,* VII, s. 1, n. 5.
[38] *De leg.,* III, c. 20, n. 5.
[39] As Suarez himself notes, the question of what is the nature of law and
obligation is ultimately the same as that in regard to prayer and vow or con-

Since obligation proceeds from the will of the lawgiver, it is his prerogative to determine whether the law will oblige *ad culpam* or *ad poenam*. If he so wills, the law obliges in conscience to the doing of what is commanded. If he does not so will, then the law obliges only to the payment of the penalty.[40] This distinction obviously is the foundation for the theory of purely penal law which Suarez held, as we shall see.

Likewise in regard to the seriousness of the obligation, this also was left to the will of the lawgiver. It was his prerogative to will whether the obligation was under pain of mortal or venial sin. Even if the matter was grave, unless the legislator willed to oblige under mortal sin, the law did not so oblige. For in such a case the only source of grave obligation is lacking, namely, the will of the superior.[41]

So in regard to civil law, Suarez takes a stand against the position of Gerson and others.[42] Civil laws do oblige in conscience, and for various reasons. First, the legislator acts through the power received from God, hence as His minister. Secondly, the divine and natural law demand

---

tract. Are they essentially of the intellect or the will? St. Thomas maintains that just as law is an act of the intellect, so also are prayer and vow. The reason is that as in law, their essence is a relation of order between the individual and God. But the establishment of this relation of order is the work of the intellect. Cf. *Sum. theol.*, II–II, q.83, a.1; q.88, a.1. Suarez, however, because he holds that *ordinare* can pertain to the will, maintains the opposite opinion: prayer and vow are of the will (*De statu religionis*, VI, lib. 1, c.13). Cf. also *De leg.*, I, c.4, n.8; *ibid.*, c.5, n.17–18; *ibid.*, c.14, n.13.

No better examples could be had—than law, prayer, vow, or contracts—of the important practical effects of profound divergences on the metaphysical level of the nature of the intellect and will.

40 *De leg.*, I, c.14, n.7.
41 *Ibid.*, III, c.27.
42 Cf. chap. 5, p. 75.

that just laws be observed. Whoever violates them acts contrary to the divine will. Thirdly, this power is necessary for the fit government of the human commonwealth.[43]

Purely penal law. But even though civil laws oblige in conscience, the question may be asked, how they may oblige. Could they oblige in conscience only to the payment of the penalty and not to the act on account of which the penalty is imposed?[44]

Aquinas, Sylvester, Soto, and Bellarmine, Suarez says, hold that there cannot be such a law. Their reasons for doing so are fourfold. First, it is of the essence of law that it oblige in conscience. Therefore a purely penal law is no law. Secondly, it is an injustice to impose a penalty without a preceding fault. Thirdly, without a preceding fault there is no reason for a greater or smaller penalty. And, fourthly, no reason can be given why certain penal laws oblige in conscience rather than others, nor can it easily be shown how such laws can be discerned.[45]

Nevertheless, in spite of such difficulties, Suarez says there can be such a law. This was also the opinion of Castro and others. For these there is the threefold distinction of law: a moral law, a mixed penal law, and a purely penal law, as Castro had previously explained.[46] Suarez, like Castro, takes issue with those who malign the notion of purely penal law. And although Navarrus says it is a new distinction and Sylvester ridicules it as puerile,

43 *Ibid.,* c. 21, n. 6–8.
44 *Ibid.,* V, c. 4, n. 1.
45 *Loc. cit.*
46 *Ibid.,* n. 2.

verbal, and useless, Suarez like Castro comes to its defense
and says it is neither new nor puerile. It was held by important doctors both modern and ancient, such as Castro
and Henry of Ghent. Nor can it be called useless or merely
verbal, because it rightly expresses a fact, the establishment of which can be effected with the best of reasons.[47]

What, then, is the underlying reason for this tripartite
division of law? It is that obligation is founded on the will
of the lawgiver and not upon the objective necessity of
means to end. It depends completely upon the will of the
lawgiver whether a law obliges to what is commanded
without a penalty, or whether it obliges to what is commanded with a penalty, or whether it obliges—not to the
act specified—but only to the payment of the penalty.[48]

The validity of such a division of law and of the notion
of purely penal law is shown by the fact, says Suarez, that it
is in accepted and approved use by religious orders. If it
should be objected that such statutes in religious orders
are not true laws but only counsels or agreements, it must
be pointed out that such is not the case. They are com-
monly considered true laws and are so called by the pontiffs who have given the power to establish them. Then,
too, because they are acts of jurisdiction and authority
imposing the necessity of acting in a certain manner, they
go beyond both counsel and mere agreement. For though
they suppose some sort of agreement in the beginning, inasmuch as a religious profession of state is necessary, yet
afterward obligation arises from the consequent jurisdic-

47 *Loc. cit.*
48 *Ibid.,* n. 3.

tion of the superior. Hence the essence of law is present if the law induces necessity either *ad culpam* or *ad poenam*. Purely penal law, therefore, obliges the subject in conscience to pay the penalty attached to the law, if he is guilty of the transgression.[49]

Hence it should be said that purely penal law always obliges in conscience, as St. Thomas holds, if not to the doing of the act specified, at least to the payment of the penalty.[50]

How can it be determined whether a law is purely penal or not? It can be known, Suarez explains, following Castro on this point, by determining what the intention of the lawgiver is. This should be discernible from the words he uses in the promulgation of the law.[51] If the words are not clear, it may be presumed to be a purely penal law, since if the law is meant to be rigorous this fact should be so stated.[52] If the words give no indication of the lawgiver's intention, the gravity of the penalty may furnish a clue.[53] Or finally, if this fails, the matter of the law should be considered. If it is something necessary for the common good, the presumption is that it is the intention of the lawgiver to oblige in conscience. Otherwise, if the matter is only civil and not of great moment, then the law is purely penal.[54] What is to be noted is that here, just as in the de-

---

[49] *Ibid.*, n.4; cf. *ibid.*, c.7, n.6.
[50] *Loc. cit.* The reference that Suarez makes here to St. Thomas (*Sum. theol.*, II–II, q.186, a.9 ad 1) is the one usually made in any attempt to find in the Angelic Doctor support for the theory of purely penal law. That this passage, if taken in context, cannot be so construed will be shown later.
[51] *Ibid.*, n.8.
[52] *Ibid.*, n.9.
[53] *Ibid.*, n.10.
[54] *Ibid.*, n.12.

termination of the gravity of the obligation, it is the intention of the lawgiver and not the matter of the law which receives primary consideration. If the matter is considered, it is only to ascertain what the will of the lawgiver should have been.

Nor does the objection hold, Suarez says, that there can be no obligation to a penalty if no fault has preceded. It is sufficient that there be a cause for the imposition of the penalty, for instance, if there is question of something that will contribute to the common good. The superior may will to bring about its accomplishment simply through fear of the penalty that must be paid if the act is not done. This would be a just cause, though not involving any fault.[55] So Suarez, again like Castro, solves the *culpa-poena* problem by allowing as valid the substitution of a *causa* for a *culpa*.

But what of the objection that, though the concept of purely penal law may be a valid one in a religious order where one may freely consent to accept a penalty even though no fault has been committed, nevertheless in the civil order an entirely different set of conditions prevails with the consequence that a purely penal civil law is impossible? [56] Suarez answers that the principles upon which purely penal law is founded in religious orders can be extended to any community or commonwealth. For in the civil community there also obtains, or there is already supposed, a pact between the individual members and the community or commonwealth to form a civil union. This

---

[55] *Ibid.*, n. 5; cf. *ibid.*, c. 3, n. 7.
[56] Cf. below, Bellarmine, chap. 12.

pact being supposed, the superior has the power to command and oblige in a way that is just and useful for the community.[57]

Suarez thus places himself in line with those who, as mentioned above,[58] see no difference in the origin of necessity and obligation in the religious union and in the civil union. For him, as for these others, the end of a religious union is primarily a common good, just as is the end of a civil union.

But a devastating consequence follows from these premises. It is that, as in a religious order many transgressions have no direct and immediate moral content, so in the civil order there are many transgressions of laws which in no way imply a moral fault. At most, such transgressions may be called only a "civil fault." [59]

In other words, there are whole sections of human civil activity that one need not bother about as directly and immediately pertaining to his conscience. It does not seem rash to venture the statement that no more complete cleavage between the moral and civil, or legal, orders could be made. Of course, grant the premised philosophy of intellect and will, then such a conclusion is consistent and inevitable. If the intellect is not allowed to present to the will the end and the objective necessity of means to the end as the principle of action, all integration of orders is impossible. For various orders of human activity can be integrated only by a proper subordination of ends. If one has accepted Suarez' teaching, from his philosophy of in-

[57] *Ibid.*, n.6.
[58] Cf. above, Henry of Ghent, chap. 1.
[59] *Ibid.*, n.13.

tellect and will down to his tripartite notion of law, one is
scarcely justified in criticizing those who (like, shall we
say, Kant who could not establish an objective end for
human activity before his ethics) maintain as basic in their
morality a fundamental distinction between the legal and
the moral orders.[60]

It helps little to say that, even though purely penal laws
do not oblige directly to what is commanded, they do
oblige indirectly, that is, to avoid contempt or disobedience. For how can a subject contemn or disobey a law that
the lawgiver himself did not intend to be obeyed in conscience? [61]

Now, as one continues to follow Suarez' thought, a suspicion begins to grow. Suarez has said that the foundation
of obligation is the will of the lawgiver. This is consistent
with and even demanded by his philosophy of intellect
and will. But along with this he has not hesitated to say
not only that law is, of course, for the common good [62] and
that there may be a *poena* without a *culpa* if there is a
cause,[63] but also that the reason why civil law obliges in
conscience when it does, is that it is necessary for the good
of the commonwealth and that if a law is not for the common good it is not a just law. Therefore it is no law.[64]
Why is this true? Because things of their very nature, of
themselves without the intention of the lawgiver, have a

---

[60] For an excellent treatment of the ultimate consequences of Thomistic,
Suarezian, and Kantian principles, see F. Ibranyi, *Ethica secundum S. Thomam
et Kant* (Rome: Angelicum, 1931).
[61] Cf. *De leg.*, III, c.28, n.21 ff., especially n.25.
[62] *De leg.*, I, c.7, n.4.
[63] Cf. above, p. 103.
[64] *Ibid.*, c.9, n.11. Cf. *ibid.*, n.12, 15.

relation to the common good.[65] In other words, although Suarez wishes to hold a subjective foundation for obligation, there is also continually creeping into his thought an objective one, the relation of means to an end.

This suspicion receives definite confirmation in Suarez' solution of the problem concerning the obligation of tax laws. After distinguishing three kinds of tax laws—real, for example, rent for land; personal, the support of the king; mixed, for instance, on imports and exports [66]—he says that laws concerning real taxes oblige in conscience. They are the matter of contract and hence pertain to justice.[67] The solution is not quite so easy in regard to the other tax laws. Ordinarily they do not oblige in conscience because they do not contain words indicating that they command the act to be done, but simply that the penalty be paid. Nor is it necessary that there be such an obligation, because the purpose of the law can be fulfilled otherwise. Thus in personal tax laws the king can be supported by the fines imposed for the nonpayment of taxes. What obligation would there be if the king no longer needed such support? Suarez' answer again finds him using an objective as well as a subjective foundation of obligation, for he says that in such event the obligation ceases either from the nature of the case, that is, because the king no longer needs support, or because the will of the lawgiver can be presumed to so intend.[68]

However, because in many tax laws there can be ques-

[65] *Ibid.*, c.6, n.9.
[66] *Ibid.*, V, c.13, n.2.
[67] *Ibid.*, n.4.
[68] *Ibid.*, n.5.

tion of matter that pertains to justice,[69] such laws are to be considered mixed laws. Why do they oblige in conscience? Because, first, their words are preceptive and the intention of the lawgiver is to acquire money necessary for the common good of the commonwealth; but also, secondly, because the matter of such laws demands an obligation in conscience, since it pertains to justice and is "necessary for the common good." In fact, such matter is "preceptive *per se* and it obliges absolutely." [70]

This most assuredly is admitting that there is certain matter which of its very nature, and not owing to the fact that it is the will of the lawgiver, has a necessary relation to an end and for that reason obliges. This is consequently admitting that the foundation of obligation is not necessarily the will of the lawgiver.

Hence it seems certain that, when Suarez applies his philosophy of intellect and will to law and obligation, he becomes inconsistent. The foundation of obligation cannot ultimately be both subjective and likewise objective. It cannot be formally both the will of the lawgiver and the very nature of the acts commanded by the law. The necessity of a certain mode of action is either based on the very nature of things or it is not. Contradictories admit only of alternate choice, but not of simultaneous acceptance.

Suarez, then, as far as our present treatment is concerned, stands at the end of the line of men who held not

69 *Ibid.,* n.7.
70 *Ibid.,* n.12.

only the primacy but even the autonomy of the will. With roots reaching back to Augustine and Anselm, the theory has developed down through Henry of Ghent, Scotus, Ockham, Biel, Castro, and finally Suarez. The intellect was not permitted a true causal part in the action of the will for fear that physical necessity would destroy freedom. But along with this went the refusal to permit the intellect to bind the will under moral necessity by allowing the intellect to present to the will certain acts as means objectively necessary for the attainment of an end. In the final fruition of this theory in Suarez, however, the objective nature of acts themselves still persisted in asserting itself with the consequence, as we have just seen, of ultimate inconsistency.

Suarez, by the very fact that he took such cognizance of it, seems to have realized the part that objective essences must play as the ultimate source of obligation. But his desire to maintain the autonomy of the will prevented him from taking a position in his psychology that would have furnished a consistent foundation for a concept of law and obligation based on objective essences.

It remained for another group of men to accomplish this. It took another approach, that of the primacy of the intellect and the mutual interaction of the intellect and will, to produce a psychology consistent with a concept of law and obligation based upon the very nature of things.

Part Two

THE PRIMACY OF THE INTELLECT IN THE CONCEPT OF LAW

CHAPTER VII

ALBERT THE GREAT

I

WHEN we begin to study the second group of men that we have chosen for consideration, we immediately feel that we are in a different atmosphere. We are on a different terrain. The distinguishing mark of a man is no longer the freedom of his will, but it is his power of intellection. To understand this position we must understand the background of the men who maintained it.

St. Albert the Great, O.P. (1206–80), can best be appreciated by considering his general approach to philosophy and theology. He is, of course, well known as the teacher of St. Thomas. Aquinas studied under him in Paris from 1245 to 1248 and in Cologne from 1248 to 1252. But this is not the reason why Albert is called "Great." His fame rests upon a much broader and more significant foundation. Albert was great because he was the first to recognize the value of Greco-Arabian philosophy for Christian theology, and this fact determined the subsequent direction of his thought.

It was during this period, as Professor Gilson says, that Christian thought finally became conscious of its profound philosophical implications and set about to formulate them in a clear and distinct way. In this Albert played a pioneer role. Ever since this time "the solidity between Aristotelianism and Christianity is such that peripatetic philosophy can be said to participate in the stability and the immutability of dogma. If scholastic theology were to be divested of its philosophical dress, one would be confronted with the theology of the Council of Nicaea and the Christian Credo." [1]

Of course profound transformations were necessary in applying such a philosophy to Christian theology. In this lay Albert's genius: he was the first to reproduce systematically, taking into account its Arabian commentators, the whole of Aristotelian philosophy, and to attempt to transform it according to the import of Christian dogma. This, then, is the background of Albert's position on the primacy of the intellect.

Intellect superior. Thus Albert speaks of the intellect as that which is the whole man. For, he says, each thing is that which is the most excellent and principal in it. Just as in a city, if one sees that the citizens are formed in virtue, he will consider the head of the city the source of this inasmuch as he has informed the citizens with his own civic virtue; so in the case of man, the intellect, which is the most excellent part of man, will inform the other parts of the soul and body according to itself. [2]

---

[1] É. Gilson, *La philosophie au moyen âge* (Paris: Payot, 1947) p. 503.

[2] *Ethic.*, X, t. 2, c. 3; Borgnet ed., VII, 628. For Albert's life and works, see H. Wilms, O.P., *Albert the Great* (London: Burns Oates and Washbourne, 1933), translated by English and Hereford. On the relation between Albert and Thomas (and their Arabian background), see M. Gorce, *L'Essor de la pensée au moyen âge* (Paris: Librairie Letouzey et Ané, 1933). For the idea of form in Albert, consult B. J. Muller-Thym, *The Establishment of the University of*

So the *esse* of man, says Albert, is not that he is a substance or that he is sensible, but rather that he is intellectual. For in all things, except for this one ultimate thing,
man is in potency. By this one ultimate thing, however,
man has his *esse* in act inasmuch as he is a man. Hence it is
proper to man that intellectual *esse* and intellectual *vivere*
are convertible.[3]

For man, then, the best and most enjoyable life is the
speculative life of the intellect. This is man at his best.
Such happiness is the highest and most worthy.[4] In fact
this life of speculation is better than the life of man itself.
If, therefore, we call the intellect divine when compared
to man, then it follows that the life of the intellect is
divine when compared to mere human life.[5]

Clearly, then, the intellect is absolutely nobler than the
will and prior to the will. For apprehension precedes all
motion of the will, but motion of the will does not precede
all apprehension.[6]

But what of the position of those who say that the will
is nobler than the intellect because virtue is in the will?
Albert responds that this is impossible. For, the *esse* of

Being in the Doctrine of Meister Eckhart of Hochheim (New York: Sheed and
Ward, 1939), chap. 2, pp. 28–67. For a survey of the nature of the Albertinian
soul, see A. Pegis, *St. Thomas and the Problem of the Soul in the Thirteenth
Century* (Medieval Studies, Toronto, 1934). For the psychology of Albert in
general, see A. Schneider, "Die Psychologie Alberts des Grossen," *Beiträge zur
Geschichte der Philosophie des Mittelalters,* Band IV (1903), Heft. 5–6, pp.
1–548.

[3] *Loc. cit.*

[4] *Loc. cit.*

[5] *Ibid.,* p. 627.

[6] *Lib. de apprehensione,* X, n.23; Borgnet, V, 676. The authenticity of the
De apprehensione has been called in question. Cf. Bourke, "The Provenance
of the *De apprehensione,*" *Speculum,* XVII (1943), 91–98. However, the work
seems at least to be of the Albertinian school.

virtue is the mean. But the mean is something that pertains to reason, and not to the will.[7]

Further, the appetitive powers cannot be the subject of virtue except so far as they participate in the form of reason. Just as perfection is in the appetite only by a reduction to reason, so there is no perfection in the moral virtues unless they are reduced to the intellectual or rational.[8]

But if this is the case, how can it be said that merit is in the will and only in the will? Albert's answer presages his position on *liberum arbitrium*. He denies that merit is in the will only. It is also in the practical judgment. It is in reason as that which determines; it is in *liberum arbitrium* as that which chooses; and it is in the will as that which completes merit by perfectly willing and acting.[9]

This last statement of Albert leaves us wondering what his position is in regard to the *liberum arbitrium*. Albert in his earlier years held that the *liberum arbitrium* was a third faculty separate from the intellect and will; he afterward abandoned this position in favor of the *liberum arbitrium* participating in both intellect and will.[10] But what eventually did Albert consider the interaction of the intellect and will to be? Did he allow the intellect, in contrast to those men whom we have thus far seen, a causal part in the determination of the will?

---

[7] *Ethic.*, VI, t.1, c.2; Borgnet, VII, 394.

[8] *Ibid.*, p. 395.

[9] *Sent.*, II, d.39, G, a.5; Borgnet, XXVII, 615.

[10] Cf. O. Lottin, *Psychologie et morale aux XII⁰ et XIII⁰ siècles* (Louvain, 1942), I, 119–27. Because Albert changed his position in regard to the *liberum arbitrium*, it was thought better in our discussion of it here not to make any references to the *Summa de creaturis*, which was written relatively early in his life, 1245–50.

From Albert's general inclination to make the intellect of prime importance, we can well expect him to give the intellect such a determining part in the action of the will. And he does so. For, as he says, the appetite in general cannot be said to be denominative of an act. It must first be determined. But the appetite cannot be determined unless through the intellect. The appetite does not move except through the form of reason. Therefore the appetite is not denominative of an act except through the form of reason, and this is called intellect.[11] So before every act of the will, the will must be informed by reason, right or wrong. "Without this information, the will is not the will, but a confused appetite." [12] In other words, the information of the will by the intellect is for Albert that without which the will would not be the will.

Now, if Albert is going to hold a mutual causality of intellect and will in the act of election, it is incumbent upon him to explain as precisely as possible in what this causality consists. This, of course, was a problem that Henry of Ghent, Scotus, Suarez, and the others, in their desire to keep the will free from any determination on the part of the intellect, never had to face. For them the intellect merely placed a condition for the act of the will. It never enjoyed a mutual causality with the will in the act of election. Therefore Albert, realizing this difficulty as implied in his position, attempts to arrive at a definite explanation.

Aristotle had said that the election was either an act of

11 *Ethic.*, VI, t. 1, c.4; Borgnet, VII, 401.
12 *Ibid.*, c. 2; Borgnet, VII, 395.

the appetitive intellect or of the intellective appetite.[13]
Now, which was it?

Albert begins by saying that, if you investigate what the
principle of action or operation is, you will find that two
things concur: namely, the determination or decree in
regard to what is to be done, and the appetite producing
the impetus to accomplish what is to be done. These two
things are found together only in the election, which is the
consiliative appetite. It is consiliative inasmuch as it dis-
cerns and commands. It is appetitive inasmuch as it causes
the impetus to accomplish the act. So the election is a
principle sufficient to explain the efficient causality of the
act.[14]

The election was, of course, for Albert not in regard to
the end, as it was for Scotus, but only in regard to the
means to the end. The will, inasmuch as it participated in
nature and was not opposed to it, necessarily willed the
end.[15]

Proceeding further, Albert explains that the election is
the selection (*praeoptatio*) [16] of one thing rather than another or others. But these two things or other things can
only be proposed by a judgment of reason. "Through
reason these things are proposed and disposed, ordered
and weighed in relation to the end intended. When one of
these has been decided and determined upon, the election
is determined and completed by the appetite giving the
impetus to accomplish the act. Hence in the election rea-

13 *Ibid.*, c.6; Borgnet, VII, 404. Cf. Aristotle, *Ethic.*, VI, lect. 2, c.5 (1139b4).
14 *Ibid.*, p. 403.
15 *Ibid.*, III, t.1, c.15; Borgnet, VII, 216.
16 Cf. below, St. Thomas, chap. 8.

son begins and disposes; the appetite terminates and completes. This is true in regard to the appetite terminated and completed." [17]

The appetite, however, which is undetermined and, as it were, diffused in regard to all things and which is the inclination of the potency to its proper act, sometimes precedes the intellect or practical reason. "For, it would neither inquire in regard to the operable, nor dispose, nor ordain, nor weigh unless it would seek or will it freely. Taken in this manner, the appetite precedes the practical intellect as a genus, whereas the intellect follows and forms the general appetite and specifies it so that it becomes the intellective appetite. Thus the appetite is the potency, and the intellect is the form and act. In this way it is properly called the intellective appetite." [18]

Hence, if the appetite is taken "in this common way,— as that which, regardless of how the appetible is shown or made known, immediately desires it before it is determined whether it is appetible or operable, or as that which does not move the first practical intellect so that by inquiring, disposing, and weighting by a judgment, it may determine, and such an operation of the soul begins in the appetite as from the imperfect and is perfected by reason discerning and determining as it does in constituting differences—then in this manner the election is the intellective appetite." [19]

If, on the other hand, the appetite is taken "as that which produces the impetus to action,—from the fact that

[17] *Ibid.,* VI, t. 1, c. 6; Borgnet, VII, pp. 403 f.
[18] *Ibid.,* p. 404.
[19] *Ibid.,* pp. 404 f.

the operable has already been determined for it by the intellect, this operation begins in the work of the intellect and is terminated and completed by the appetite—then in this sense the election is the appetitive intellect. Here the operation of the intellect is as genus and potency, whereas that of the appetite is as difference and act." [20]

In other words, when the appetite is considered in relation to the act of determining which of two or more should be accepted, the will is as potency and material cause, and the intellect is as act and formal cause. When, on the other hand, the appetite is considered in relation to the impetus to action, the intellect is as potency and material cause, and the will is as act and formal cause. The similarity between this explanation by Albert in terms of material and formal causality and Thomas' explanation of the election and the command in the same terms is, of course, more than merely coincidental. [21]

It is of great importance to note that Albert never once loses sight of the fact that the principle of the act of election is man. It is man, with his faculties of intellect and will, who elects. [22] This fact was lost sight of in the succeeding centuries when it was said that the will alone, with its power of perceiving and ordaining, elected. There is no danger of making the will itself a supposit, if it is considered as acting necessarily *with* the intellect. The supposit, man, remains inviolate in Albert.

---

20 *Loc. cit.*

21 Cf. below, St. Thomas, chap. 8. The probability is that Aquinas as well as Albert profited greatly by the work of Philip the Chancellor (d. 1236). Cf. Lottin, *op. cit.*, I, 77, note 3; 251, note 2.

22 *Ibid.*, p. 404.

Albert has taken his position. A mutual causality exists between the intellect and will. The will is determined by the intellect. Physical necessity has not been ruled out, but its action is in terms of material and formal, not efficient, causality. Therefore the way has been left open for moral necessity to be imposed upon the will by the intellect. So Albert can say that the election is mixed, in which one faculty is "the form and act of the other." Hence it may be said that the election is of the will inasmuch as "the will is informed by reason judging." [23]

From what Albert has just said, two difficulties arise. First, is the act of the will taken as intellective appetite really different from the act of the will taken as appetitive intellect, and secondly, which of these is the command? The answer to these questions seems to be, first, that there is a difference in these acts, and secondly, that the latter act is the command.

Command: of the intellect. Two acts seem to be involved, because Albert, following John Damascene and Gregory Nazianzen, says clearly that "after the election there is the impetus to action." [24] If this is the case, if one follows the other, then there must be two acts.

That the second act, that of impetus, was for Albert the command is equally clear from his statement that the impetus is "of reason through the command." Hence, "after the election there is the command of reason to execute what has been elected. By means of the command

23 *Ibid.*, III, t. 1, c. 16; Borgnet, VII, 218.
24 *Ibid.*, I, t. 3, c. 5; Borgnet, VII, 36.

the object is obtained. And this is called the impetus to action." [25]

Does Albert say that the impetus is the command of reason because of the formal election of order that must be contained in it? It is hard to find him saying so explicitly. But what he does do is clearly imply that, because the impetus-command directs the powers to carry out the action, the idea of *ordinare* is therein contained. For Albert all order that the will may have must come from reason. Only reason can establish order. "It pertains to the reason to order (*ordinare*) the will." It is the intellect, then, which directs and orders all things.[26] Hence, because the impetus in question is not blind, but is ordered to the end, it must pertain to the intellect. Command is, therefore, of the intellect. Albert was the first, so it seems, to identify the *impetus* of John Damascene with the command of reason.[27]

With the command established as an act of the intellect, Albert's position in regard to law is already indicated.

II

Law: of the intellect. The definition of law that Albert uses most frequently is that of Cicero: "Law is written justice which commands what is right and forbids what

[25] *Sum. de creaturis*, II, q.69, a.2; Borgnet, XXXV, 566.

[26] *Evang. Matthaei*, VI, n.10; Borgnet, XX, 276. Cf. *Ethic.*, I, t.5, c.1; Borgnet, VII, 57; *Sum. de creaturis*, II, q.65, a.2 ad q.3; Borgnet, XXXV, 552.

[27] *Sum. de creaturis*, II, q.69, a.2; Borgnet, XXXV, 566. As one author says: "We have already noted that the commentary of Albert on the text of Damascene is distinguished by the emphasis placed upon its rational aspect" (F. M. Drouin, O.P., "Le libre arbitre selon Albert le Grand," *Publications de l'institut d'études médiévales d'Ottawa*, I–II [1932], 97). Cf. also Lottin, *op cit.*, I, 412.

is wrong and threatens punishment to those who transgress." [28] Law must, of course, be for the common good,[29]
and its purpose is to produce citizens who are good.[30]

Albert does not seem to be concerned about directly
defining law in terms of an act of the intellect or will. The
closest he comes to it seems to be a remark made by way of
comment on Cicero's definition. Here he says that law is
the "form of justice which is educed from the form which
is in the mind of the king, committed to writing for the
ruling of the people." [31] But of course Albert had already
said that the "precept is the command," [32] and that the
"command pertains to reason." [33] Hence there can be no
doubt that for Albert law was the command of reason.

However, further confirmation of the fact that law was
for Albert an act of the intellect and not of the will, is not
lacking.

First, he says that by positive law universal principles
are applied to particular cases. But such an application of
the universal to the particular can only be "accomplished
by reason." [34] Only the intellect can perceive the relation
between the universal and the particular.

28 *Evang. Matthaei*, VI, n.10; Borgnet, XX, 267. (The reference to Cicero is
Rhetoric, Bk. I, ad fin.) Cf. *Ethic.*, V, t.3, c.3; Borgnet, VII, 369.

29 *Ethic.*, V, t.3, c.3; Borgnet, VII, 367.

30 *Ibid.*, I, t.9, c.1; Borgnet, VII, 140.

31 *Evang. Matthaei*, VI, n.10; Borgnet, XX, 267.

32 *Compendii theologicae veritatis*, V, n.59; Borgnet, XXXIV, 192. It is true
that Albert sometimes says that the precept is a sign of the will. But he is
careful to explain that it is not merely the will, but the will commanding
which is in question (*Sum. theol.*, I, t.20, q.80, n.1; Borgnet, XXXI, 863).
Hence such a sign is of the "will in reason."

33 Cf. above, p. 119.

34 *Sum. de creaturis*, II, q.71, a.1; Borgnet, XXXV, 593. Cf. *Ethic.*, X, t.3,
c.3; Borgnet, VII, 640.

Secondly, Albert says that law is the mean of justice. For, the determination of what is just is the determination of the mean. But, as he has already said, to determine the mean is a work of reason involving, as it does, the perception of a relation. Therefore law must be an act of reason.[35]

Thirdly, in explaining *epikeia* Albert indicates that law is of reason. For, he says, *epikeia* is really an extension of law. Like law, it is a direction of means to the end in cases not covered by the law itself. But such direction demands a judgment of reason. Hence both *epikeia* and law itself are acts of reason.[36] And what will determine this judgment in regard to relation of means to the end? The objective relation of the means to the end. Reason will judge according to the nature of the acts involved.[37] Albert has already indicated his foundation for obligation.

Obligation: from the nature of the act. In regard to obligation, then, Albert says that a definition of precept, inasmuch as it is obligatory, would be: "A precept is a command, obliging to the observation of the act commanded on account of the authority of the one commanding or the nature of the thing commanded." [38] According to this, the foundation can be both the authority of the lawmaker and the nature of the thing commanded. Suarez said that the foundation of obligation was the will of the lawgiver; then afterward he allowed the nature of the act

[35] *Politicorum*, III, t. 10, dd; Borgnet, VIII, 307.
[36] *Ethic.*, V, t. 4, c. 1; Borgnet, VII, 384. Cf. also *ibid.*, p. 386.
[37] *Ibid.*, p. 384.
[38] *Sent.*, III, d. 37, A, a. 2; Borgnet, XXVIII, 680.

also to have a part. Now, is this not precisely what Albert is doing? He says that the obligation of the command comes both from the authority of the one commanding and from the nature of the thing commanded. Prescinding from the problem of obligation in religious orders, Albert's statement can stand and contains no inconsistency in regard to the foundation of obligation in the civil order. Why? Because for Albert the judgment of the one in authority had to be based on the nature of the act. For Albert the will was not independent of the intellect. It was its nature to be "in the judgment of reason." And the judgment of the intellect had to be in accord with objective reality. It was a property of the intellect to be a judge, but the judgment must conform to the order and truth of things.[39] Hence, for Albert to say that obligation comes from authority and the nature of things, is not to oppose but to include the one in the other. This he can do because his psychology warrants it.

In Albert, then, we find a man whose endeavor was to explain the function of the intellect and will in terms of mutual causality, formal and material. He was not preoccupied with preserving the freedom of the will from any physical necessity that might be imposed by the intellect. For him the one was somehow "in" the other. The link between the will and objective reality was the intellect. Hence the way was open for law to be an act of the intellect, and for the foundation of obligation to be reality itself, not the will alone.

[39] *Sum. de creaturis,* II, q.70, n.2; Borgnet, XXXV, 578; cf. *ibid.,* p. 576.

It is true that Albert's philosophy of intellect and will as well as his concept of law was not fully developed. Nor was the relation between the two fully noted and pointed out. That remained for his pupil to accomplish: Thomas Aquinas.

CHAPTER VIII

THOMAS AQUINAS

I

St. Thomas Aquinas, O.P. (1225–74), carried on and completed the work that his master had begun, namely, the methodical transformation of philosophy and theology according to the principles of Aristotle. Consequently, as far as our present problem is concerned, Aquinas will hold the primacy of the intellect. In maintaining this position, however, he was accused by his adversaries of failing to vindicate free choice. His principles, they said, led to the will being necessitated. This was as bad as Averroism. Hence the condemnation of 1270 and 1277, though explicitly aimed at Averroism, implicitly included St. Thomas.[1] The effect of this seems to have been that St. Thomas felt it necessary, not to change his position, but to clarify it. His stress was henceforth not so much on final as on formal causality.[2] It is according to this clarification, then, that we shall study Aquinas' philosophy of intellect and will.

Intellect more noble. For St. Thomas, then, the intellect is nobler than the will. This is true for several reasons.

[1] Cf. above, chap. 1.
[2] Cf. O. Lottin, *Principes de morale* (Louvain: Mt. César, 1947), II, 16–19.

Because powers are specified by the objects of their acts, if the object is nobler, then the power is nobler. This is the case in regard to the intellect. Its object is nobler than that of the will because it is more simple and absolute. The object of the intellect is the form or essence itself of the appetible good; the object of the will is this appetible good which has its form in the intellect. Hence, absolutely speaking, the intellect is nobler than the will.[3]

Relatively speaking, however, that is, in relation to the difference in objects themselves, the will may be said to be higher than the intellect. This is based on the nature of the operation of the intellect and will. The operation of the intellect is perfected by the presence of the object known in the intellect. Hence the nobility of the operation of the intellect is in proportion to the nature of the intellect. But the operation of the appetitive is perfected by the inclination of the appetite to the object as to its term. Therefore the dignity of the operation of the will depends on the nature of the object of the operation. From this it follows that those objects which are less noble than the soul are in the soul in a nobler manner than in themselves. For each thing is in another according to the nature

---

[3] *Summa theologiae*, I, q. 82, a. 3, c. In regard to the authenticity of the title *Summa theologiae* rather than *Summa theologica*, see A. Walz, "De genuino titulo Summae theologiae," *Angelicum*, XVIII (1941), 142–51. According to this author the title *Summa theologica* seems to have made its appearance first sometime about the sixteenth century. On the other hand, the oldest manuscripts of Aquinas' work, the custom of his times, and the fact that there have never been lacking those who did employ it when speaking of this work, would serve to indicate that the genuine title is *Summa theologiae*.

The best works on St. Thomas, as far as our present problem is concerned, seem to be those of O. Lottin, *Principes de morale* (Louvain: Mt. César, 1947) and *Psychologie et morale aux XIIe et XIIIe siècles* (Louvain: Mt. César, 1948), and those of A.-D. Sertillanges, *S. Thomas d'Aquin* (Paris: Alcan, 1925) and *La philosophie morale de S. Thomas d'Aquin* (Paris: Alcan, 1946).

of that in which it is. So it is nobler to have knowledge of those objects which are beneath us than to have love of them. On the other hand, it is better to have a love of those objects which are above us, rather than merely to know them.[4]

Hence, in regard to inferior objects the intellect is nobler, in regard to superior objects the will is nobler. But prescinding from this difference in objects and considering the powers in themselves, as mentioned above, the intellect is nobler than the will.[5]

Or, to put it another way, the intellect is nobler than the will because of the manner of operation of each, because the perfection and dignity of the intellect consists in the presence of the form of the thing known in the intellect itself. It is by this that the intellect knows, and this is its whole dignity. But the nobility of the will and its act consists in the fact that the soul is ordered to some noble object according to that which the object is in itself. Now, it is more perfect, absolutely speaking, to have the nobility of another thing in yourself than to be ordered to a noble object existing outside yourself. Hence, if the intellect and will are considered in themselves and not in regard to this or that object, then the intellect must be said to be more eminent than the will.[6]

But is not the will a higher power than the intellect, since it is the will that moves the intellect to act?

St. Thomas, even in regard to motion, is careful to maintain the pre-eminence of the intellect. For, he says,

[4] *Loc. cit.* Cf. *ibid.*, II–II, q. 23, a. 6 ad 1; *ibid.*, I–II, q. 3, a. 4 ad 4.

[5] *Loc. cit.* Cf. *Scriptum super sententiis, In III Sent.*, d. 27, q. 1, a. 4, c.

[6] *Quaestiones disputatae, De veritate*, q. 22, a. 11, c.

it is the intellect that first moves the will. For the will, as will, is moved by its object, which is the apprehended good. But the will can be regarded as moving the intellect inasmuch as the act itself of knowing is apprehended as good and is desired by the will, from which it follows that the intellect actually knows. And in this the intellect precedes the will. For the will would never desire the act of knowing if the intellect did not first apprehend the act of knowing as good.[7]

Besides, continues St. Thomas proving the same point, the will moves the intellect to action just as an agent is said to move; but the intellect moves the will after the manner in which the end moves. For the known good is the end of the will. But an agent in moving is posterior to the end because the end is that on account of which the agent acts. Therefore it is evident that the intellect is, absolutely speaking, higher than the will. The will can be said to be higher than the intellect only relatively,[8] that is, inasmuch as motion pertains to the will by reason of its object.[9]

For St. Thomas, then, the intellect is in general nobler than the will. But one thing must be noted. This superiority is not established by instituting an independence of one from the other. Rather they are repeatedly spoken of as including one another. The intellect knows that the will wills, and the will wills that the intellect knows. Similarly the good is contained under the true inasmuch as it is known, and the true is contained under the good inasmuch as it is a good desired.[10]

[7] *Summa contra Gentiles,* III, c. 26, ad 5.
[8] *Loc. cit.*
[9] *De verit.,* q. 22, a. 12 ad 5.
[10] *Sum. theol.,* I, q. 82, a. 4 ad 1.

Now, if St. Thomas is going to hold an interaction of the faculties of intellect and will, then it behooves him, as it did Albert, to explain exactly what sort of causality is involved. Undoubtedly influenced by Albert and perhaps also by Averroes,[11] Thomas proceeds to explain this interaction in terms of formal and material causality. As a matter of fact, he applies this explanation much more extensively than is generally realized. It is not only the key to the solution of the vexing problem of the election and the command—which immediately concerns us here—but also of the problems of the relation between the proximate and ultimate objects of the human act,[12] between the command and the commanded acts,[13] and between *caritas* and the other habits.[14]

Thomas' general position, then, in this regard is that whenever two powers act together, that which is from the superior power is as form to that which is from the inferior power which is as matter.[15] That is, when there is question of an act which is composed of the acts of inferior and superior powers, that of the inferior will be as matter to that of the superior, which will be as form.[16] Of course this composite act is truly one act, since the act of the one moving and of the one moved is one act.[17]

[11] Averroes had said that in every action produced by two diverse powers, "it is necessary that one of the two be as matter and instrument and the other be as form and agent" (*In 3 De Anima,* text c. 36 [Juntas ed.], Vol. VI, I, 2, f. 184c).

[12] *Ibid.,* I–II, q. 18, a. 6, c.

[13] *Ibid.,* q. 17, a. 4, c.

[14] *Ibid.,* II–II, q. 23, a. 8, c; *De verit.,* q. 14, a. 5, c. Cf. G. Klubertanz, S.J., "The Unity of Human Activity," *The Modern Schoolman,* XXVII (1950), 75–103.

[15] *De verit.,* q. 14, a. 5, c.

[16] *Sum. theol.,* I–II, q. 17, a. 4, c. Cf. *ibid.,* III, q. 19, a. 2, c.

[17] *Ibid.,* a. 4 ad 2.

Command: of the intellect. What is the result of the application of this principle of material and formal causality to the problem of the act of command? Does the act of commanding pertain essentially to the intellect or to the will?

Before discussing the act of command, let us first see what the effect of this principle is in explaining the election. The root of freedom, Aquinas says, is in the intellect. The will is free to be directed to different objects "because the intellect is capable of different concepts of the good." Therefore the intellect is the cause of liberty. Liberty is rooted in the intellect.[18] Is election therefore an act of the intellect? The first thing to be decided is: To which faculty does election belong essentially? Which faculty elicits the act? Aquinas says election is essentially an act of the will because the perfection of the election comes from the motion of the soul to the good which is chosen, and this motion is, of course, from the will.[19] But what of the fact that the root of liberty is in the intellect: that the intellect is the cause of liberty?

It is in answer to this otherwise insoluble difficulty that Aquinas applies the principle of mutual interaction of material and formal causality. He says that reason can be said to precede the will and order its acts inasmuch as the will tends to its object according to the order of reason, because the apprehensive power presents its object to the appetite. Hence "the act by which the will tends to something which is proposed as good, by the very fact that it is

---

18 *Ibid.,* a. 1 ad 2. Cf. *De verit.,* q. 24, a. 2, c.
19 *Ibid.,* q. 13, a. 1, c. Cf. *De malo,* q. 6, a. un., c.

ordered to an end by the intellect, is materially of the will
and formally of the intellect." [20]

Therefore the election is essentially an act of the will;
but when considered in relation to the intellect it is materially of the will and formally of the intellect.

It seems that unless this explanation is admitted, true
causal interaction of the intellect and will is impossible,
and only the autonomous will of Scotus and Suarez is
left.

Now, what of the command? Is it the same act as the election, as in Ockham, Biel, and Suarez? Is it a separate act? Is
it of the intellect or will?

Aquinas says clearly that the command is an act of the
intellect which *follows* the act of election, in regard to
one's self or others.[21] This means that "the command
is essentially an act of reason, because the one commanding orders (*ordinat*) him whom he commands. . . .
To order thus pertains to reason." [22] The will is incapable
of establishing order between one thing and another—in
contrast to what Scotus and Suarez taught. Only the intellect, which can perceive a relation, is capable of establishing order.[23]

But the intellect elicits the act of ordering and directing
only in virtue of the previous act of election. The command is an act of the intellect, but presupposing an act of
the will.[24] It is through the election that the intention

20 *Loc. cit.*
21 *Ibid.*, q.17, a.3 ad 1.
22 *Ibid.*, a.1, c; cf. *ibid.*, II-II, q.83, a.1, c. That by "reason" Aquinas means
in this context "intellect," see below, chap. 6, note 22.
23 *In IV Sent.*, d.15, q.4, a.1 ad 3.
24 *Sum. theol.*, I-II, q.17, a.1, c.

of the end and the impetus thereunto is carried on.[25]

Therefore the command is of both the intellect and the will. It is of the will inasmuch as it implies an inclination or motion. It is of the intellect inasmuch as this inclination or motion is ordered and directed to execution by this or that power.[26]

The command, then, like the election is a composite act of intellect and will. But which is its formal and which its material aspect?

Aquinas answers this question by determining which is the superior power in the act of command, the intellect or will. The intellect is the source of the order in the command, and the will is the source of the motion. But inasmuch as the ordering to the end presupposes the desire of and motion to the end, the principle of command, that is, that from which it has its inception, is the will. In this sense, then, the will may be called superior. Therefore, according to St. Thomas' principles, if the will is superior, its act is as form to the act of the intellect, whose act is as matter.[27]

Therefore the command is essentially an act of the intellect, but when considered in relation to the will it is materially of the intellect and formally of the will.

It is in the light of this explanation that all those statements of St. Thomas must be interpreted and under-

---

[25] *In IV Sent., loc. cit.*

[26] *De verit.*, q. 22, a. 12 ad 4. Cf. *Quodl.*, IX, q. 5, a. 12, c.

[27] *In II Sent.*, d. 25, q. 1, a. 2 ad 4; cf. *In IV Sent.*, d. 15, q. 4, a. 1, sol. 1 ad 3. Although St. Thomas does not explicitly use the words "form" and "matter" in regard to the command as he does in regard to the election, their use seems not only justified according to the principles he has laid down, but even desirable. Cf. below, chap. 9, for Cajetan's contribution in this matter.

stood wherein he says command is of the will. True, he says this many times.[28] But it must always be remembered that when he precisely determines what the command is, he says it is essentially an act of the intellect.[29]

With this fact firmly established, it is but a short step to its application in determining the nature of law.

II

Law: act of the intellect. For St. Thomas law is essentially the act of command. And because command, as we have seen, pertains to the intellect, so also does law. Law is an act of the intellect.[30]

Why is law the act of command? Because law is essentially the ordering and directing of means that lead to an end. That is why law is a rule or measure of what must be done in order that the end may be attained.[31] But such an ordering and directing is, psychologically considered, the act of command. Therefore law is the command, and the command is law.

Hence the moving, ordering, and directing of others by those in authority are done by the command of law.[32] This is, of course, analogous to the command which an individual person gives to himself.[33] If one speaks of the command as "the will of the superior," it must be understood as the motion of the will ordered and directed by

28 Among others, for instance: *Sum. theol.,* I, q.21, a.2 ad 1; *ibid.,* q.107, a.1, c; *ibid.,* II–II, q.4, a.2 ad 2; *ibid.,* q.10, a.2, c; *ibid.,* q.166, a.2 ad 2; *De malo,* q.2, a.2 ad 1; *In II Sent.,* d.40, q.1 a.5, c.
29 *Sum. theol.,* I–II, q.17, a.1.
30 *Ibid.,* q.90, a.1, sed contra.
31 *Ibid.,* a.1, c.
32 *Ibid.,* II–II, q.50, a.1, c; cf. *ibid.,* q.104, a.1, c; *ibid.,* q.102, a.2, c and ad 3.
33 Cf. *ibid.,* I–II, q.17, a.1, c; *ibid.,* II–II, q.50, a.2, c.

the intellect, as explained above. Otherwise there is no
question at all of a law which is a good, but rather of
violence and therefore something evil.[34]

The purpose of law is to attain an end. It is on account
of an end that law commands necessary means.[35] And since
law is of its nature directive of the man, the end that law
is intended to accomplish must be of its essence communi-
cable to many. Therefore the end of law is a common
good.[36]

Hence St. Thomas' classical definition of law: "an ordination of reason for the common good by him who has
the care of the community—promulgated." [37] In other
words, law is for St. Thomas an authoritative ordering on
the part of an intellect of means necessary for the attainment of a common good.

Upon this basic concept of law, is based St. Thomas'
analogy of law.[38] In every instance it is the act of an intellect in authority ordering means to an end. The eternal
law is the divine intellect ordering all things to one final
end.[39] Granted the act of creation, all things must somehow participate in this primordial ordering.[40] They will
participate in it passively inasmuch as their forms, irra-

34 *Ibid.*, I–II, q.96, a.4, c. Cf. *ibid.*, q.90, a.1 ad 3; *ibid.*, q.93, a.3 ad 2.
35 *Ibid.*, q.90, a.2, c.
36 *Loc. cit.* Cf. *ibid.*, ad 2, 3; *ibid.*, q.96, a.1, c.
37 *Ibid.*, q.90, a.4, c.
38 The problem of the analogy of law in St. Thomas is well set up by M.
Adler ("A Question about Law," *Essays in Thomism* [New York: Sheed and
Ward, 1942]). The solution arrived at, however, is questionable.
39 *Ibid.*, q.91, a.1, c; cf. *ibid.*, ad 3; *ibid.*, q.93, a.1, c. St. Thomas says that
the divine will could be called the eternal law, but only in the sense that what
God wills in regard to creatures is contained in the divine wisdom. For this
reason the will of God is called reasonable (*ibid.*, q.93, a.4 ad 1).
40 *Ibid.*, q.93, a.2, c.

tional or rational, bespeak this divine ordering and constitute what is called the natural law, both physical and moral.[41] Such a law is law, therefore, only by an analogy of attribution. Or they will participate in this ordering actively inasmuch as by their own intellectual power they authoritatively order means to an end. This latter participation is obviously the prerogative of only those creatures whose form is intellectual. Hence such laws as are established by human authority are laws by an analogy of true proportionality.[42] From this the analogous nature of law and the common good is evident.

Obligation from relation of means to end. In his explanation of the derivation of law Aquinas has said that *lex* comes from *ligando* because it obliges.[43] What is the source of this obligation? What is the foundation of obligation for Aquinas? Is it in the will of the lawgiver, as it was for Scotus and Suarez? Or is it in objective reality as presented to the will by the intellect?

In discussing the fact that law must be just if it is to be a law at all, Aquinas says that just laws oblige in conscience. Why? Because they are ordinations to an end, the common good. Hence for Aquinas obligation seems to have its foundation in the objective relation of the means ordered to the common good.[44] A law obliges because what it commands is for the common good.[45]

---

41 *Ibid.,* q.91, a.2, c; cf. *ibid.,* q.90, a.1 ad 1.
42 *Ibid.,* q.91, a.2 ad 3.
43 *Ibid.,* q.90, a.1, c.
44 *Ibid.,* q.96, a.4, c.
45 *Ibid.,* a.6, c.

But do not, for instance, Suarez and others quote this same passage, use these same words, and still maintain that the foundation of obligation is the will of the law-giver, rectified though it may be according to what is for the common good? What assurance is there that St. Thomas held a moral necessity which was founded in things?

Besides what would seem to be the obvious meaning of his unqualified statement just mentioned (that laws oblige because of their relation to the common good), it is abundantly clear from his explicit treatment of necessity that for Aquinas the foundation of obligation is objective reality.

Aquinas says necessity can be of several kinds. In general that is necessary which cannot not be. Now, this may derive either from an intrinsic principle or from an extrinsic principle. From an intrinsic principle necessity may occur either on account of a material cause, as when we say that it is necessary for things composed of contraries to corrupt; or on account of a formal cause, as when we say that it is necessary that a triangle have three angles equal to two right angles. From an extrinsic principle necessity may arise either on account of an agent, as when one is forced by someone to do something that he would not otherwise do, and this is called necessity of coaction; or "on account of an end, as when an end cannot be attained without this means. . . . This is called necessity on account of the end." [46]

But is it this type of necessity, namely, that on account

46 *Ibid.*, I, q. 82, a. 1, c.

of the end, that is imposed by the command of law? What Aquinas has said thus far already contains the answer: Yes. But if an explicit statement to this effect is sought, it is not hard to find. Aquinas says it is this kind of necessity—conditioned necessity, or necessity on the supposition of an end—that is imposed by the command of the lawgiver. Just as corporeal action binds corporeal things with physical necessity of coaction, so the command of the lawgiver binds the will of the subject with moral necessity based on the objective relation of means to an end.[47]

So it is the command that indicates those things which are morally necessary, that is, without which the end cannot be attained.[48] That is why Aquinas explains the basic command of the natural moral law in terms of the end. He says that, "because good is the end of the appetite, the intellect naturally apprehends the end of the appetite as indicated by the inclinations as good, and consequently as that which must be done." [49] In other words, from these principles it follows that necessity on condition of the end, or moral necessity or obligation, is as immediately known as is the nature of things. The foundation of obligation is the relation between created forms. That is why from an immediate knowledge of this first principle which includes a concept of necessity based upon conditions of an end, the end—God—can be proved to exist.[50] Deny this, and an essential part of the preamble of faith cannot

[47] *De verit.*, q. 17, a. 3, c.
[48] *Ibid.*, q. 23, a. 3, c.
[49] *Sum. theol.*, I–II, q. 94, a. 2, c.
[50] Cf., for instance, Cajetan, *Comm. in Sum. theol.*, In I–II, q. 71, a. 6, and Boyer, *Cursus philosophiae* (Paris: Desclée, 1937), II, 337.

be proved from reason. Before it can be said that man is obliged to believe God on divine authority, man must first have a concept of obligation. It must first be shown that man is obliged to do what is good for him according to the demands of his rational form, for this is what will lead to his end.[51] If the existence of God must first be known before the concept of obligation, then "Good must be done" is not a first principle.

Obligation may therefore be said to be for St. Thomas, the moral necessity of placing certain acts imposed upon the will by the intellect perceiving that these acts are necessary means to a necessary end.

Could Scotus or Suarez accept such a definition of obligation? Evidently not, because for them the intellect presenting objective reality is incapable of any true causal relationship with the will. Hence obligation must be founded in the will. In Aquinas, however, such is not the case. The intellect does have a causal part in the action of the will. Because of this, the intellect can impose upon the will the moral necessity—not physical, of course—of placing certain means that it perceives are necessary to attain a certain end. The foundation of this moral necessity imposed upon the will by the intellect is, therefore, ultimately the order of created forms or essences as perceived by the intellect.

Praecipere seu imperare? Attention should be called here, perhaps somewhat parenthetically, to something

---

[51] For the relation of man's rational form to his end, see *Sum. theol.*, I–II, q.21, a.1; q.71, a.2.

that has been the cause of great confusion: St. Thomas'
use of the words *praecipere* and *imperare*. Do these words
refer to one and the same act, or do they refer to different
acts? Do they both mean "command"? Cajetan and Medina
say one thing; Soto says another.[52]

No one can deny that St. Thomas does speak at times as
if they were synonymous.[53] But if his complete treatment
of the matter is taken into consideration, it will be evident
that *praecipere* and *imperare* refer to different acts.

For the *praecipere* is before the election or rather part
of it,[54] whereas the *imperare* is after the election.[55] If this
is the case, then evidently they cannot be the same act.

But if the *praecipere* is part of the election, just what is
it? Is it a "command" of the intellect that leaves the will
no choice but to obey? Taken in this sense it is the *bête
noire* against which Scotus and Suarez were ever at war.
Or is it, on the other hand, an act of the intellect imbued
with the will, so that ultimately it is a judged election or
an elected judgment? Taken thus, it is the composite act
of St. Thomas with its material and formal aspects. It is
not a "command" at all, but a *judicium electionis*.[56] The
word *praecipere*, then, used to denote the act of the intel-

---

[52] Cf. below, Cajetan, chap. 9; Soto, chap. 10; Medina, chap. 11.

[53] For instance, in *Sum. theol.*, I–II, q.12, a.1, c; *ibid.*, q.90, a.1, sed contra; *ibid.*, q.92, a.2, c; *ibid.*, II–II, q.47, a.8, 3 Praeterea; *ibid.*, q.104, a.4, c; *ibid.*, a.5, c; and *De verit.*, q.17, a.3, c.

[54] *Ibid.*, I–II, q.58, a.4, c. Cf. also *De virt. in com.*, q.un., a.12 ad 26; *In III Sent.*, d.33, q.2, a.3, c; *In VI Ethic.*, lect. 9, Pirotta 1240; *ibid.*, lect. 11, Pirotta 1290; *Sum. theol.*, I–II, q.57, a.6, c; *ibid.*, II–II, q.47, a.1 ad 2.

[55] *Ibid.*, q.17, a.3 ad 1. Cf. *De verit.*, q.22, a.12; *Quodl.*, IX, q.5, a.12; *In IV Sent.*, d.15, q.4, a.1, quᵃ 1 ad 3.

[56] *De verit.*, q.24, a.1 ad 17. Cf. *ibid.*, q.23, a.8 ad 4; *Sum. theol.*, I, q.86, a.1 ad 2: *ibid.*, I–II, q.76, a.1, c; *ibid.*, II–II, q.47, a.3 ad 1.

For one of the best expositions of St. Thomas' judgment of election, see A.–D. Sertillanges, *S. Thomas d'Aquin* (Paris: Alcan, 1925), II, 267.

lect before or with the act of election, seems to derive from
prae-accipere, which in turn St. Thomas uses as practically
synonymous with *prae-eligere.*[57] Hence the word *praecipere,* if used to denote the act of the intellect in the election, is better translated as the "judgment of election"; if
it is used to denote the act of the intellect that directs
execution after the election, then it is synonymous with
imperare and should consequently be translated as "command."

It could well be asked, if St. Thomas meant two different
acts by *praecipere* and *imperare,* why did he so often use
them together? One answer might be that, although they
are separate acts psychologically, they are never separated
practically. Whenever there is an efficacious election to
act, the command, directing the powers to carry out this
act, must follow.[58] Hence *praeacceptio* or *electio* is always
present with the *imperium.* Then too it may be added, as
many times seems to be the case, St. Thomas may have
used *praecipere* as synonymous with *imperare* meaning,
as just explained, the command after the election.

Purely penal civil law? With law, therefore, having as its
purpose the accomplishment of an end by the use of means
that are necessarily related to this end, and obligation hav-

---

[57] For instance, in *De virt. in com.,* q.un., a.12 ad 26, he says: . . . *praecipere
sive eligere quod facit prudentia.* In *Sum. theol.,* I–II, q.13, a.2, c, he says:
. . . *cum electio sit praeacceptio unius respectu alterius,* and in *ibid.,* q.15,
a.3 ad 3: . . . *ex multis praeaccipimus unum eligendo.* . . .

[58] Hence the acts of the habits of *eubulia, synesis,* and *gnome* have to do
with the essence of law; whereas those of prudence have to do with its *esse.* Cf.
Sum. theol., I–II, q.57, a.6, c; *ibid.,* II–II, q.47, a.2 ad 2; *ibid.,* a.8, c; also L.
Thiry, O.S.B., "Speculativum et Practicum secundum St. Thomam," *Studia
Anselmiana* (Rome: Herder, 1939).

ing this very same relation of means to the end as its foundation, the question of whether all true laws oblige in
conscience to the act specified seems superfluous. If man
is obliged to use the means necessary to his end, and law
is concerned only with such means,[59] then law must oblige
in conscience. So St. Thomas in answer to the question,
"Do human laws oblige in conscience?" says without
qualification that they do.[60]

But could this mean that laws oblige in conscience in
one of two ways: either to what is specified or to the payment of the penalty? In other words, did St. Thomas hold
that a purely penal civil law was possible?

The answer to this question is threefold: first, if he did
hold that purely penal civil law was possible, he never explicitly said so; secondly, such a concept is against his principles of law; and thirdly, the attempts to make him say so
implicitly are taken from discussions about religious or
ecclesiastical law.

What is to be made of the fact that St. Thomas, like his
teacher St. Albert, makes no explicit mention of purely
penal civil law? Henry of Ghent, a contemporary of both
Albert and Thomas, had spoken of it, though for Henry
purely penal civil and religious law were to be treated as
one. Had Albert and Thomas not heard of purely penal
civil law? Or, if they did hear of it, why did they not treat it?

Regardless of what the truth of this matter is, the concept of purely penal law is against the principles of law
that Thomas has established. If law, to be just, has to be

59 *Sum. theol.*, I–II, q.96, a.2, c.
60 *Ibid.*, a.4.

concerned directly only with what is necessary for the common good, and man is obliged in conscience to do what is necessary for the common good, then there is no choice: all laws oblige in conscience directly to what is specified, namely, to that which is necessary for the common good.

The passages usually referred to by those who seek to find the concept of purely penal law in St. Thomas are principally two, both in regard to the religious or ecclesiastical order.

First, in discussing whether a religious always sins mortally in transgressing what is in the rule,[61] Thomas answers simply: No, every transgression is not a mortal sin. Some may be venial sins. In fact, he says, in some religious orders, like the Order of Preachers, some transgressions do not oblige even under pain of venial sin, but only to the payment of the penalty imposed, because the rules oblige to observation in this manner.[62] Now, this is clearly the notion of purely penal law in a religious order. No one certainly would take exception to this, because in a religious order the subject has agreed to be obliged primarily, not in regard to those things which are necessary for the common good, but in regard to whatever the superior may judge to be for his own individual good. The "watering of a dry stick" has no direct relation at all to the common good, but it does have an immediate relation to the individual good of the one enjoined by obedience to water it.

But it is in answer to the second objection to this same

---

[61] *Ibid.*, II–II, q.186, a.9.
[62] *Ibid.*, ad 1.

article that we find the phrase which some believe shows that St. Thomas held the notion of purely penal civil law. The objection made, says St. Thomas, is that rules are imposed on religious in the same manner as a law. But whoever transgresses the command of law sins mortally. Therefore it seems that the monk who transgresses the rule sins mortally.[63] St. Thomas answers that not all things contained in law are given as a command, but some things are proposed as a sort of ordination or statute obliging only to a penalty. Just as in civil law transgression of a legal statute is not deemed worthy of corporeal death, so in ecclesiastical law all ordinations and public statutes do not oblige under pain of mortal sin. Similarly not all statutes of the rule of a religious order oblige under pain of mortal sin.[64]

That this passage does not prove that St. Thomas held purely penal civil law can be shown from these considerations. First, the law about which he is directly speaking is the rule of a religious union. That is demanded by the context. For, he says, among the things contained in the "rule" are those things that oblige on account of the religious vow. Hence, when he says that not all things contained in the law are given as a command, but some are proposed as "ordinations" or "statutes," it must be understood in regard to law in a religious order. Secondly, he is principally concerned with the question of whether religious rules oblige under pain of mortal sin. Hence, when he refers to civil law he does not say that just as civil law sometimes

[63] *Ibid.,* 2 Praeterea.
[64] *Ibid.,* ad 2.

obliges only to the penalty, so also the rule of religious orders. But what he does say is that just as civil law sometimes does not make the transgression worthy of death, so also the rule of religious orders does not always oblige mortally. Whether civil law may oblige only to the payment of the penalty is here left unconsidered. Hence this passage is not concerned with the question of purely penal civil law.

The second passage sometimes referred to as showing that St. Thomas held the concept of purely penal law is in regard to the question whether, without a dispensation, all are bound to the fast instituted by the Church.[65] In explaining the fact that exceptions can be made in certain cases, St. Thomas says that this is possible because it was not the intention of the legislator that his command be always observed, except in cases where it will promote greater good.[66] For, he says, the command of the legislator does not oblige when it nullifies his intention. The intention of the legislator is to conserve men and make them good. If the law does not conduce to this end, then it does not bind, and superiors may dispense.[67]

It should be evident that the phrase "intention of the lawgiver" in this passage refers, not to the lawgiver's intention to oblige to the act specified or the penalty, but to his intention of obtaining the end. This passage is not concerned with the foundation of obligation; it is about the foundation of *epikeia,* which, as judged by superiors,

[65] *In IV Sent.,* d. 15, q. 3, a. 2, sol. 1.
[66] *Loc. cit.* Cf. *ibid.,* sol. 2.
[67] *Ibid.,* sol. 4.

is dispensation.[68] Hence, to say that because Aquinas uses the phrase "intention of the lawgiver" in regard to *epikeia* and dispensation, means also that he was referring to the source of obligation, is to confuse two separate questions: the extent and interpretation of any given law and the nature of law itself.[69]

So, it is certain that St. Thomas did not hold the notion of purely penal civil law. Such a notion is contrary to his principles of law and his philosophy of intellect and will. That such is the case is now being gradually recognized.[70]

Of course this is only consistent with St. Thomas' more general principle that any transgression of a temporal law has eternal implications.[71] A transgression of the temporal law is a sin against the eternal law because the former is but an expression of the latter, just as an act which is against the work of an artist is against the artist himself.[72] The *peccatum philosophicum* is, therefore, unintelligible according to these principles. True, not every observance of civil law is meritorious: that depends upon the presence of sanctifying grace. But on the other hand, no observance

---

[68] Cf. *Sum. theol.*, I–II, q.96, a.6; *ibid.*, II–II, q.120, a.1, 2.

[69] Compare *Sum. theol.*, I–II, q.90, with *ibid.*, q.96, a.6.

[70] As one author says, the attention of Thomists holding purely penal law should be called to the fact that "this error is intolerable. For Suarezians, who hold that law is the work of the will, at least logic is preserved. But for Thomists, who say that law is the work of reason and who hold that the end (or the common good) founds and orders all morality,—the very existence of society, the union of men, authority, law, and all other things—the holding of purely penal law is something incomprehensible. Nor should it be said that the statutes of many religious institutes are purely penal laws. . . . Because even if this were true, which we would not concede, such statutes should be called simply non-laws, rather than purely penal laws" (M.–C. Gonzales, O.P., "De imperfectione morali," *Etudes et recherches, théologie*, Cahiers II–III [Ottawa, 1944], p. 323, note 1).

[71] *Sum. theol.*, I–II, q.71, a.6 ad 5.

[72] *Ibid.*, a.2 ad 4.

or transgression of civil law is without a moral implication. Human acts may be indifferent to supernatural merit
for the reason just given, but they are not indifferent to
goodness or badness, for their immediate end stands somehow or other in relation to the ultimate end.[73] When St.
Thomas speaks of a civil act, he means one that may or
may not be meritorious.[74] But when Suarez, for instance,
speaks of a civil act, he means one that may or may not
have moral content—an entirely different thing.[75] For St.
Thomas every act, if it is a true human act, has moral implications: it is good or bad in some sense.

St. Thomas gives us, then, the first comprehensive treatment of law that is integrated with a philosophy of intellect and will.

Because in his psychology there is in the election and
the command a mutual interaction of formal and material
causality, St. Thomas has no false problem of the freedom
of the will versus the physical necessity of the intellect. As
a consequence of this, when it comes to moral necessity,
the intellect is not impeded from imposing upon the will
the necessity of acting according to the demands of the
objective relation of means to an end.

Since only the intellect is the cognitive faculty, and
order and direction must come solely from it, law is an act
of the intellect. Laws oblige in conscience because they

---

[73] *Ibid.*, q. 18, a. 9, c.

[74] Even an act which is good only civilly, like any naturally good act, may
help dispose one in the state of mortal sin for the reception of sanctifying
grace. Cf. *In II Sent.*, d. 40, q. 1, a. 5, sol. and ad 5; *ibid.*, d. 41, q. 1, a. 2, sol.

[75] Cf. above, Suarez, chap. 6.

simply specify means that lead to an end that man, by his very nature, is already obliged to work for. There are no indifferent acts in the concrete. And since laws thus oblige, the concept of a purely penal civil law is foreign to the thought of St. Thomas.

Because of his philosophy of intellect and will, then, St. Thomas' concept of law and obligation is based upon the objective nature of things.

CHAPTER IX

THOMAS DE VIO (CAJETAN)

I

Thomas de Vio (Cajetan), O.P.[1] (1469–1534), was a man of transition. Reared in the philosophy and theology of the Middle Ages, he found himself in the midst of a full-blown intellectual and religious revolution. His desire to defend the traditional doctrine accounts for one preoccupation in his writings: the refutation of Lutheranism.

The other subject that occupied a great part of Cajetan's attention was Scotism. Cajetan taught the doctrine of St. Thomas at Padua from 1493 to 1496, and at Pavia from 1497 to 1499. During his stay at Padua he came into close contact with living Scotism, especially in the person of the able Franciscan, Trombetta. As a consequence large portions of Cajetan's writings are given over to a refutation of Scotism and—what particularly concerns us here—voluntarism.

Cajetan's work is all the more important because of the great influence he had on Vitoria, one of the so-called "founders of international law." [2]

Cajetan's concept of law and his philosophy of intellect

---

1 Capreolus was omitted here because his *Defensiones* yields too little on law as such.
2 Cf. below, chap. 10, note 3.

and will are, then, in the main those of St. Thomas. His interest for us, consequently, lies principally in his interpretation of St. Thomas. This is also true of the rest of the men whom we shall consider. Some of their interpretations seem to be in the authentic line of St. Thomas' thought, at least as it is beginning to appear today. Other interpretations seem to have given cause for the violent opposition that developed against the so-called "Thomist" position.

Intellect more noble. Cajetan, like St. Thomas, holds that the intellect is without qualification the nobler faculty because the object of the intellect is nobler than the object of the will. This is true because it is more simple and more absolute. The object of the will is the good, yet the very form or essence of the good is in the intellect. But the form of a thing is more simple and absolute than that of which it is the form. Hence, since the essence of a power is determined by order to its object, the intellect must be nobler than the will.[3]

Relatively speaking, as St. Thomas had said, the will may be said to be nobler than the intellect. For the object of the will is sometimes found in a higher thing than the object of the intellect. The object of the will is in things; the object of the intellect is in the soul. Therefore sometimes the object of the will is a nobler thing than the object

[3] Cajetan, *Commentaria in summam theologicam S. Thomae,* I, q.82, a.3; Leonine edition, V, 299.

For the life, works, and influence of Cajetan, see the special number of the *Revue Thomiste,* XXXIX (1934–35), 1–503. Cf. also A. Touron, *Histoire des hommes illustres de l'ordre de Saint Dominique* (Paris, 1743), IV, 1–76.

of the intellect. For instance, the love of God is nobler than a knowledge of Him, but knowledge of corporeal things is nobler than a love of them. Hence the will may sometimes be said to be nobler than the intellect. But absolutely speaking, as explained above, the intellect is nobler than the will.[4]

If the intellect is nobler than the will, to which faculty does the prerogative of establishing order pertain? As for St. Thomas so also for Cajetan, to order and direct can be an act only of the intellect. Cajetan is vehement in rejecting the "Scotistic fantasy" that *ordinare* pertains to the will either according to its nature or inasmuch as it participates in the intellect.[5]

For, whatever there is of order in natural things or in voluntary acts proceeds from reason and is resolved into it. The work of nature is the work of intelligence: a principle according to which, from the order in things, it is possible to prove the existence of a supreme ordering Intelligence. This is true also of the act of election in which order especially appears. Election is of those means which lead to an end. But counsel, which is an act of the intellect, establishes this order between the two. The will then, when it chooses, inclines to these means according to the order of reason. It is the intellect which directs to the end, whether truly or falsely, implicitly or explicitly, formally or virtually. Hence all order that appears in the will is perfectly resolved into that which proceeds from the intellect. Then too, that the establishment of order and direction is

[4] *Loc. cit.*
[5] *Ibid.*, I–II, q. 17, a. 1; VI, 119.

the work of the intellect is the common conception of the mind.[6]

Command: of the intellect. If the establishment of order is thus the unique function of the intellect, then what is the command, which is composed of order and motion? Is it of the intellect or of the will?

Cajetan's approach to this problem is the same as his approach to the election,[7] which is also that of St. Thomas. Each problem is solved by applying the principle of material and formal causality to composite acts.

Though the command is composed of order and motion, and is therefore of both intellect and will, to which does it pertain essentially? The answer is not difficult to find. If the essence of the command is order, and order is an act only of the intellect, then the command is essentially of the intellect. But what of the motion with which this order is composed? What part does the will play? Applying the principle that the superior power is as form to the inferior power which is as matter, Cajetan determines which of the two is the superior power in this composite act of command. He says that in the command the will is the superior power. Why? Because it is the principle of motion, the *primum movens,* without which there would be no action for the intellect to direct to an end.[8]

Hence the command, because it is an ordering, is essentially an elicited act of the intellect. When taken, however, in relation to the motion with which it is composed, the

[6] *Loc. cit.*
[7] *Ibid.,* q.13, a.1; VI, 98.
[8] *Ibid.,* q.17, a.1; VI, 119. Cf. above, St. Thomas, chap. 8.

order of the intellect stands as matter to the motion of the will, which is as the form.

It is to be noted that Cajetan seems to be one of the first to use the words "matter" and "form" explicitly in regard to the command. St. Thomas, as will be remembered, while explaining the command according to the principles of matter and form, does not use the words "matter" and "form." This seems to have been an obvious and authentic completion that Cajetan made.[9]

In regard to the words *praecipere* and *imperare*, Cajetan uses them as synonymous, as did St. Thomas at times, to denote command.[10] But he says that it can be both before [11] and after [12] the election.

Cajetan, realizing that there seems to be an inconsistency lurking here,[13] attempts to explain why he can say that *praecipere seu imperare* is before the election and that it is also after the election. He says that *praecipere seu imperare* can be understood in two ways: first, in regard to the election absolutely, that is, in regard to that which

---

[9] How did Cajetan intend the words "matter" and "form" to be taken here? Up to this point he seems to mean the words to be taken literally, as St. Thomas did. However, two passages cast some doubt upon this. In one (*ibid.*, q.58, a.5; VI, 378) he says that the command is an act of the intellect formally and of the will virtually; whereas the election is an act of the appetite formally and of the intellect virtually. Why does Cajetan oppose "virtually" instead of "materially" to formally? Has he shifted from actual composition to a "composition" by extrinsic denomination?

Again, in another passage (*ibid.*, q.95, a.2; VII, 176) Cajetan says that positive law determines the natural law as form determines matter. But actually such a determination of natural by positive law is a specific determination of a common genus. Is Cajetan here reducing formal and material causality to logical concepts?

[10] *Ibid.*, q.17, a.1; VI, 119. Cf. *ibid.*, II–II, q.47, a.6; VIII, 354; *ibid.*, I–II, q.58, a.5; VI, 377.

[11] *Ibid.*, p. 378.

[12] *Ibid.*, II–II, q.47, a.6; VIII, 354. Cf. *ibid.*, I–II, q.16, a.4; VI, 117.

[13] *Ibid.*, q.88, a.1, n.2; IX, 235.

a person commands himself to elect. Taken in this sense, the command is the final act of practical reason before action. Or, secondly, command can be taken in another sense, that is, in regard to others. A person may command something to his subjects; taken thus, command is distinguished from entreaty and promise. For command pertains to inferiors, entreaty ordinarily pertains to superiors, and promise refers to all. Hence these three acts are distinct from the command taken in the first sense. For command in the first sense is rectified by prudence and is the cause of the election; command in the second sense, along with entreaty and promise, is the effect of the election.[14]

What Cajetan has done here is to confound an already confused question. Instead of showing that *praecipere seu imperare* before the election cannot mean a true command on the part of the intellect to the will, he attempts to say that there are two commands, one before and one after the election. (That by *praecipere seu imperare* he means, not the judgment of election of St. Thomas, but true command, is shown by the very expression he uses: *praecipit sibi ipsi eligere*.) If the intellect commands the will to elect, as Cajetan is here trying to say, then there is only one conclusion possible: the will is no longer free to elect.

It is such statements as these, later repeated by others,[15] that gave men like Suarez every justification for saying that the "Thomistic" doctrine on intellect and will destroyed liberty.[16]

[14] *Loc. cit.*
[15] Cf. below, Medina, chap. 11.
[16] *Disp. metaph.*, XIX, c.6, n.2, E.

However, though Cajetan is not too successful in his explanation of the election and the command, he holds that the *praeceptum seu imperium* pertains to the intellect. It is this which becomes the foundation for his concept of law.

II

Law: an act of the intellect. Cajetan's position on law is, as we have noted, in its main outlines that of St. Thomas. Law is that act of the intellect which needs only the motion of the will in order that it be law.[17] But such an act of the intellect is, as we have just seen, the command, receiving its motion from the previous act of the election. Therefore law is the command of the intellect.

The concept of law is analogous, as explained above.[18] Divine providence directing all things to the ultimate end is the eternal law. This is participated in by rational and irrational creatures.[19] Hence the eternal, natural, and human law may each be said to be, in its own individual way, the divine governance of all things.[20] Human positive law consists in the specific determination of what is contained in the natural law in general.[21]

Of course, law must be for the common good. It is essentially related to this objective end. What is not for the common good does not have the force of law.[22] In fact, this

---

[17] Cajetan, *op. cit.,* I–II, q.90, a.1; VII, 150. Cf. *ibid.,* q.58, a.5; VI, 378, and note 9 above.
[18] Cf. above, St. Thomas, chap. 8.
[19] *Ibid.,* q.91, a.1; VII, 153; cf. *ibid.,* q.93, a.3; VII, 164.
[20] *Ibid.,* a.3; VII, 155.
[21] *Ibid.,* q.95, a.2; VII, 176.
[22] *Loc. cit.* Cf. *ibid.,* q.96, a.4; VII, 186; *ibid.,* q.99, a.3; VII, 242.

is the basis for a distinction that may be made between law and precept. Law is an ordering to the common good, whereas precept is concerned with individual ends and goods that are subordinated to the common good. If such a subordination is not present, there is no question of a true precept.[23]

This stress on objective finality in the nature of law bears good fruit for Cajetan when he applies it to the difference between the civil order and the ecclesiastical or religious order. For he says that the precise difference between the two is: The end of the civil order is the objective common good of all; the end of the religious order is the internal good of the individual person.[24] With this distinction so clearly established, Cajetan is well on the way to an understanding of law and the foundation of obligation in the civil order as distinct from "law" and the foundation of obligation in the religious or ecclesiastical order. This is a definite step forward.

Obligation: from order of means to the end. What is the foundation of obligation? Cajetan says that law has the force of obligation in general from the eternal law.[25] In law there are two forces: one directive and one coercive. The directive is in regard to the acts commanded; the coercive is in regard to the penalty inflicted.[26] This directive to the common good, which is law, derives ultimately from the authority of the eternal law.[27] So, when the legis-

23 *Ibid.*, q.90, a.2; VII, 151.
24 *Ibid.*, II–II, q.63, a.3; IX, 64.
25 *Ibid.*, I–II, q.96, a.5; VII, 185.
26 *Loc. cit.*
27 *Ibid.*, p. 185.

lator makes a law, the cause of the obligation which the law induces is twofold: the will of the legislator to make the law, and the eternal law. This will of the legislator is not the will to choose freely to oblige or not to oblige, because a legislator has no such choice. It is rather his will to make the law. For, by the very fact that he wills to promulgate the law, he also wills that the ordination have the force of law and oblige. Therefore the act of the will in question here is the act of deciding that the law is necessary. But an ordination, that it may oblige and direct conscience, must derive from the eternal law. Hence the obligatory force of law comes from the eternal law as from a universal cause, and from the will of the legislator to pass the law as from one determining this universal cause to a special effect.[28]

Now, how does the obligatory force of law come from the eternal law? This is a point which Cajetan does not explain very well. His excursus into the physical science of his day does not help much. He says that as the bones of an animal are produced by Saturn, so the obligatory force of law is communicated by God.[29] This hint at reification of a concept like obligation is, to say the very least, very misleading. Obligation cannot be communicated like a physical effect. For obligation is moral necessity imposed upon the will. Hence the way the obligatory force of law derives from the eternal law is still not explained by Cajetan.

He does say clearly that obligation is founded on the order to the end: that it is the objective relation of means

[28] *Ibid.*, p. 186.
[29] *Loc. cit.*

to end which is the basis for moral necessity.[30] He says further that "the will can will something on account of end or supposition. This is proved, because when an end can be attained by one means only, the will is necessitated to this one means." [31] To integrate this with the eternal law, all Cajetan needed to do was to show that creative essences, the result of the divine creative act, manifest such an ordination to an end. Then obligation based on the necessary order of essences to the end would have to be from the eternal law.

Why did not Cajetan see his way clear to say this? It may be ventured that it was because he was too much under the influence of certain ideas prevalent at his time, ideas which did not come from St. Thomas. If the foundation of obligation is based on the objective order to the end, as Cajetan said, this objective order must be of essences. It is the essence of an act that has a relation to an end, even before it is made the matter of law. Cajetan seems to have wavered on this, wrongly relating the distinction between the indifference of the human act *in specie* and *in individuo* to the distinction between the speculative and the practical intellect.[32] For, the relation between an act and the end on account of which it is placed is the proper consideration of the speculative intellect alone. The practical intellect decides to do or not to do the act in order to attain this end.[33]

---

[30] *Ibid.*, II–II, q.147, a.3; X, 157.
[31] *Ibid.*, I, q.82, a.1; V, 294. This, it may be well to note, is Cajetan's only comment on *necessitas ex suppositione finis,* a most important part of this article of St. Thomas. Cf. above, chap. 8.
[32] *Ibid.*, I–II, q.95, a.2; VII, 176. Cf. *ibid.*, q.96, a.4; VII, 184.
[33] Cf. St. Thomas, *Sum. theol.*, I–II, q.57, a.6, c, and II–II, q.47, a.8, c.

In spite of this lapse, the principle of finality is still strong enough in Cajetan to form the basis for distinguishing the necessity of various types of human activity. On this basis Cajetan distinguishes, as did St. Thomas, mortal from venial sin, and precept from counsel.[34] And because, as we have seen above, Scotus had said that mortal sin is distinguished from venial sin inasmuch as one is against a precept and the other against a counsel, Cajetan takes this opportunity, when speaking of the part finality must play, to take him to task for his "most false" statement.[35]

Laws, then, for Cajetan oblige in conscience because of their nature they are an ordering to an end. Therefore they oblige under mortal or venial sin.[36]

Purely penal law? But could there be a law which obliged only to the payment of the penalty, a purely penal law? What Cajetan held on this point is not absolutely certain. What is certain though, is that he did not attempt to interpret St. Thomas in favor of purely penal civil law.

When he comments on the passage mentioned above (the one wherein the proponents of purely penal civil law usually try to find support in the Angelic Doctor),[37] Cajetan explicitly says that this passage refers to law in a religious order. When the word "law" is given a particular meaning, he says, subsequent conclusions in regard to it

[34] *Ibid.*, II–II, q. 104, a. 2; IX, 386. Cf. *ibid.*, q. 88, a. 2; IX, 239; *ibid.*, q. 147, a. 3; X, 157; *ibid.*, I–II, q. 72, a. 5; VII, 18.
[35] *Ibid.*, I–II, q. 72, a. 5; VII, 18. Cf. *ibid.*, q. 96, a. 4; VII, 184.
[36] *Ibid.*, II–II, q. 104, a. 3; IX, 388.
[37] Cf. above, St. Thomas, chap. 8.

should be drawn accordingly.[38] That "law" in this passage refers to the law or rule of a religious order is shown from the context, especially since it includes whatever comes under the religious' vow of obedience.

Now, according to his vow the religious may agree to oblige himself to receive from the superior, without having committed any fault, whatever inflictions the superior may judge to be contributive to the individual's own perfection. Therefore, because of his voluntary subjection to the superior in this matter, the principal obligation of the rule is, Cajetan says, in regard to the acceptance of these penalties. Therefore the religious rule does not directly oblige *ad culpam,* but only *ad poenam.* And, because strictly speaking there can be no true punishment without a preceding fault, the *poenae* referred to really are certain inflictions that the superior judges good for the inferior.[39] For these reasons, then, the purely penal law that is discussed in this passage is that which pertains solely to the "law" or rule of a religious order with its unique aspect that comes from the vow of obedience. Hence, as far as Cajetan's comment is concerned, no conclusion may be deduced from it in regard to purely penal civil law.

The fact that Cajetan does not seem to hold purely penal civil law receives further confirmation from the way he explains the obligation consequent upon a true command. For he says that, though all commands do not oblige under pain of mortal sin, that does not mean that they do not

---

[38] *Ibid.,* q. 186, a. 9; X, 502.
[39] *Loc. cit.*

oblige under pain of sin at all. They may, in fact, oblige under pain of venial sin.[40] This is true of many acts of temporal civil life.[41]

Cajetan, then, was a man who, because he held the primacy of the intellect and attempted to hold the mutual interaction of the intellect and will in terms of formal and material causality, was able to maintain with consistency that law was the command and therefore an act of the intellect; and he was able to hold that obligation was based on the objective relation of means to an end.

True, Cajetan in his explanation of some of these points leaves much to be desired. The full part that essences and finality play in the explanation of order and the eternal law does not receive the prominence it should. Even his explanation of the interaction of intellect and will makes one think at times that he was reading thirteenth-century pages exclusively through sixteenth-century eyes.

Whether Cajetan was a true witness to the authentic thought of St. Thomas is a judgment that others will have to pass. For our present consideration, he is a man who did hold, in general, a concept of law and obligation that was founded upon and consistent with his philosophy of intellect and will.

40 *Ibid.*, p. 502.
41 Cf. *ibid.*, II–II, q.88, a.2; IX, 239. For Castro's attempt to make Cajetan hold purely penal civil law, cf. below, chap. 5.

CHAPTER X

DOMINIC SOTO

I

DOMINIC SOTO, O.P.[1] (1494–1560), is of value for our present study because his work is indicative of how St. Thomas was being interpreted at one of the great centers of the sixteenth-century Thomistic revival, Salamanca. Vitoria, who as mentioned above was greatly influenced by Cajetan,[2] was the main inspiration of this revival, and became known as the *"Instaurator Sancti Thomae"* and as one of the founders of international law. Soto taught at Salamanca with Vitoria from 1532. Though perhaps not seeing or expressing the relation between the concept of law and the philosophy of intellect and will as clearly as Medina (whom we shall consider in the next chapter), Soto does appear to have grasped it better than did Vitoria.[3] And al-

---

[1] Sylvester Ferrara, O.P. (1474–1526), has been omitted because he has too little on our problem to warrant inclusion here.

[2] Cf. above, chap. 9.

[3] The main reason why Francis Vitoria, O.P. (1480–1546), was omitted from consideration here is that his philosophy of law seems to be at variance with his psychology. Thus, in his psychology he follows St. Thomas and holds that the intellect is the superior faculty—with all the consequences that this entails (*De eo ad quod* [Lyons, 1586], pp. 335 f.). But in his treatment of law he abandons these principles and embraces the primacy of the will, saying that the will of the legislator may take the place of reason: *Sufficit voluntas legislatoris, cum sit pro ratione voluntas (De potestate civili* [Madrid, 1934], n. 16, p. 197). Further work should be done on Vitoria to determine his place as an authentic Thomistic commentator.

though it is true that some statements that he makes [4] seem to warrant his inclusion among the men of the opposite group,[5] which we have already considered, yet, as we shall see, a closer inspection of his psychology and his philosophy of law seems to justify his being placed in the present group.[6]

Intellect more noble. Soto follows St. Thomas in holding that the intellect is a nobler faculty than the will. For, the good of the intellect is, absolutely speaking, better than the good of the will.[7]

To the intellect also belongs the prerogative of directing, as well as of knowing. For this reason the will can hardly be called the queen, and the intellect the servant. For the will of itself is a blind power. Its illumination and direction must come from the intellect.[8] Hence for Soto the intellect is nobler than the will.

Command: of the intellect. With the intellect thus endowed with the power of directing, it follows that the command pertains to the intellect. The will elects, and after this the intellect commands.[9]

The series of acts leading to the command, then, is as

[4] Cf. below, note 57.
[5] Cf. for instance, Suarez, *De legibus,* V, c.4, n.1; Vangheluwe, "De ortu atque profectu sententiae disiunctivae in explicanda lege pure poenali," *Miscellanea Moralia* (Louvain, 1948), I, 212.
[6] Cf. below, p. 176.
[7] *De justitia et jure,* III, q.4, a.4 (Bertani edition), p. 238. For information on Soto's life, works, and importance see De Heredia, "El Maestro Domingo (Francisco) de Soto," *La Ciencia Tomista,* XLIII (1931), 357–73, and the same author, "Soto," *Dictionnaire de théologie catholique,* XIV (1941), 2423–31.
[8] *Ibid.,* I, q.1, a.1, p. 5. Compare with Henry of Ghent above, chap. 1.
[9] *Ibid.,* p. 6.

follows: Those things which are conducive to the end desired are sought out by the intellect through the first habit of prudence, *eubulia*. These are then approved by a judgment through the second habit *synesis*. Next they are elected by the will. Finally, the command of prudence immediately follows. This command is a proposition, not of the indicative mood, but of the imperative: this is to be done or avoided.[10]

Or, to put it a little more specifically in terms of means and end, *eubulia* is concerned with inquiring into the means that will lead to the end; *synesis* judges rightly about these means. Then, besides these acts, is required the act of prudence, the command, which is uniquely ordered to action.[11]

It is worth noting that Soto, like St. Thomas, Cajetan, and Medina, uses the words *praecipere* and *imperare* throughout, interchangeably.[12] Does this mean, however, that like Cajetan and Medina, Soto is also going to say that *praecipere seu imperare* is had both before and after the election?

Soto saw the consequences of a command before the election more clearly than Cajetan or Medina did. He saw that if there were a true command before the election,

10 *Ibid.*, p. 5.
11 *Ibid.*, p. 4. That Soto should connect St. Thomas, *Sum. theol.*, I–II, q.57, a.6 (the *praecipere* of prudence) with *ibid.*, q.17, a.1 (the *imperium* which follows the election) is extremely interesting. (Cf. above, St. Thomas, chap. 8.) There are those who say that never once did St. Thomas in his treatises on prudence make "even an allusion" to the *imperium*. He always used the word *praeceptum*. Cf. Lottin, *Principes de morale* (Louvain: Mt. César, 1947), I, 254, note 2. While this is for the most part true, there is an exception. Cf. *Sum. theol.*, II–II, q.47, a.8, 3 Praeterea.
12 *Ibid.*, I, q.1, a.1, *passim.*

then the liberty of the election would be destroyed. So, to avoid such a fatal predicament, he insisted that there could be no command before the election. The only act of the intellect before the election was the judgment of *synesis*. This sufficed for the election.[13]

But this election was not sufficient for action.[14] Although a man, after the judgment of *synesis*, might elect a good work, still, as experience shows, even after such an election he might be slow and sluggish in putting it into action. For, as Soto continues to explain, many elect in their minds to lead a very holy life, who nevertheless, because of the slowness of the command of prudence, enter upon it most tardily.[15]

If this is the case, then how did a man dispose himself to act readily? Was another habit needed which would dispose to prompt, efficacious election? This was a real difficulty, and his opponents seized upon it immediately and held that no act of the intellect was possible after the election.[16] They argued: If the command follows the election, as Soto said, then it must do so necessarily or freely. It could not follow necessarily, for then there would be no further need of the virtue of prudence to command, as Soto was holding. But this was against Aristotle and the very truth itself. Nor could the command follow freely, for then the election of the will would not be enough, and another act would be needed. This again was against what

13 *Ibid.*, p. 6.
14 *Loc. cit.*
15 *Ibid.*, p. 5.
16 *Ibid.*, p. 6. Compare with Suarez, above, chap. 6.

Aristotle and St. Thomas and all other philosophers had ever taught.[17]

How does Soto attempt to extricate himself from this difficulty? He says, first, that "neither does the command follow necessarily from the election, nor is any other act required in the will besides the election." [18] Why? Because, since in order that one power be moved by another it is necessary that each be well disposed, it follows that unless the election is sufficiently well rooted and the intellect well prepared by prudence, the command will not follow from the election. Therefore, "where the election is solid and strong and the intellect sufficiently acquiescent, the command immediately follows the election." Otherwise, it follows with difficulty or not at all.[19]

In other words, if the dispositions which are required in order that the command follow the election are not present, the command does not necessarily follow. This means only that there is still need of another habit of election that disposes to an efficacious election to act, from which the command must necessarily follow. Soto's adversaries are still unanswered.[20]

What Soto did not see was that the habit of prudence itself is the habit which disposes to the election to act,[21] from which necessarily follows the command to the inferior powers directing them in the execution of the means

[17] *Loc. cit.*
[18] *Loc. cit.*
[19] *Loc. cit.*
[20] Cf. above, St. Thomas, chap. 8, pp. 130 f. and 139 f.
[21] St. Thomas, *Sum. theol.,* I–II, q.57, a.4, c.

elected. Because he failed to see this, he did not answer the dilemma of his adversaries.

Soto, then, in his philosophy of intellect and will does two things principally. First, in opposition to Cajetan, he allows no command before the election, saying that the judgment of *synesis* suffices; and secondly, he says that the command follows the election but fails to show how it does so, necessarily or freely.

The result of this is: first, in the act of election the causality of the intellect is not assured, since the judgment of *synesis* is not causally related to the act of election; and secondly, there still remains the need, if Soto's explanation is accepted, of a habit disposing to the election to act. This latter is evident since for Soto the election is in regard to the specification of means and prudence is in regard to the command directing the execution of these means, with no provision being made for a habit of election to act.

Once again one can scarcely criticize Soto's adversaries for taking the position they did, confronted as they were with such an interpretation of St. Thomas' doctrine.

Nevertheless Soto, seeing the need of an act of the intellect after the election to direct the execution of the means elected to the end and believing he had vindicated such in the act of command, already had established his foundation for the concept of law.

II

Law: act of the intellect. For Soto, then, law is the command. But the command is an act of the intellect. Therefore law is an act elicited by the intellect.[22]

Law, he says, is a rule of right and wrong, a measure of action. Such a rule, however, can pertain only to the intellect. For there is question in law of direction to an end and, since the will itself is blind, such direction must come from the intellect. And because the end is the principle of human actions, the act of the intellect ordering means to an end is a rule, and therefore a law.[23]

As to the intellect itself, law is a universal proposition or dictate of the practical intellect. Of course, in the intellect there are simple apprehensive propositions as well as judicative propositions. Law, however, is not only an apprehension. It is a preception which follows the judgment: not any judgment but one which pertains to all. This is called the practical judgment.[24]

Soto proceeds to locate the command in the prudential series. First, he says, by *eubulia,* the first habit of prudence, an inquiry is instituted in regard to those things which will lead to an end. Then through the habit of *synesis,* the second habit of prudence, these are judged as to their relative appropriateness. Thirdly, the will chooses one of these. Finally, the command of prudence follows. This is not a proposition of the indicative mood, he repeats, but of the imperative: "This is to be done or not to be done."

22 *De just. et jure,* I, q.1, a.1, p. 4.
23 *Loc. cit.*
24 *Ibid.,* p. 5.

For, expressions such as "It is good to do this" are speculative propositions. They do not have the force of law. But
when they have the force of the future participle, then
they are practical dictates. And if they are dictates of the
one in authority and are promulgated to the people, then
they are laws.[25] It is this act of direction on the part of the
one in authority which constitutes law. Because only the
intellect can know and therefore direct, this act of command pertains to the intellect.[26] Therefore in God the
eternal law is in the divine intellect, not in the divine will.
For, as Soto has already said, it is the function of the intellect to illumine and direct.[27]

Hence the expression, "That which pleases the prince
has the force of law," should not be taken to mean that the
will of the prince is law. It means only that there is no law
in the prince's intellect until after there has been an election in his will. This act of the will is not law, but if that
which pleases the prince is afterward in his intellect and is
promulgated, then that is law. So, law is not the election,
but it is that which follows the election.[28]

The justness of a law is determined, says Soto following
St. Thomas, by its causes: final, efficient, material, and
formal. Stressing immediately the final cause, he says that
law must be for the common good. In fact this is the determining factor between good government and tyranny.[29]

Law therefore can be defined as a rule directing to the

[25] *Loc. cit.*
[26] *Ibid.*, p. 6.
[27] *Ibid.*, p. 5.
[28] *Ibid.*, p. 6.
[29] *Ibid.*, q.6, a.4, p. 46. Cf. *ibid.*, X, q.3, a.1, p. 921.

common good. Stressing the importance of the principle of finality in any series of causes, Soto says that the very essence of law lies in its direct relation to the end of the commonwealth, that is, the common good.[30]

Obligation: from the nature of acts. But why do human laws oblige? John Gerson had said that human laws of themselves have no obligatory force; this was true only of divine laws.[31] So, if human laws do oblige, do they oblige because of the will of the lawgiver or because of the nature of law itself as relating essentially to the end, the common good? [32]

Soto admits that this is a difficult question to solve.[33] If you say that laws oblige on account of the will of the lawgiver, then civil laws will never oblige in conscience, because in the promulgation of law it is never stated that they oblige in conscience. If, on the other hand, you grant that obligation comes from the very nature of law itself, it would follow that no lawgiver could make a law which did not oblige in conscience. This would be hard to accept, especially since in religious orders, such as the Order of Preachers, there are many laws which do not oblige in conscience.[34]

Nevertheless, in spite of these difficulties, Soto takes his stand alongside St. Thomas and concludes that civil laws oblige in conscience and they do so even to the extent of

30 *Ibid.*, I, q. 1, a. 3, p. 9.
31 *Ibid.*, q. 6, a. 4, p. 48.
32 *Ibid.*, pp. 47 f.
33 *Ibid.*, p. 46.
34 *Ibid.*, p. 48.

obliging under grave sin. For, he explains, in both the ecclesiastical and the civil unions it is necessary that laws oblige in conscience. Why? Because the whole purpose of authority and therefore of laws in these unions is to bring about the accomplishment of "the end on account of which they were instituted." [35] Since, therefore, one is obliged in conscience to work for these ends, for this same reason one is obliged in conscience to place the means that will lead to the end.

Soto, however, clearly distinguishes the manner in which authority is communicated to the ecclesiastical and the civil union. The ecclesiastical union receives authority from Christ Himself, whereas authority is communicated to the civil union through the "law of nature." [36] Just how this is done through the "law of nature" Soto does not see fit to explain further.

Of course this authority derives ultimately from above. Its ultimate purpose is not simply the temporal peace of the civil union. This proximate end tends to the ultimate end, which is eternal happiness. Hence, with the relation between the temporal and the eternal orders thus perfectly established by reason of the proper subordination of their ends, Soto can say that all law, of either order, obliges in conscience.[37]

Hence, to transgress a civil law, if it is just, is a matter of conscience and therefore of sin.[38] In such a doctrine as Soto's there is no place for the *peccatum philosophicum*.

[35] *Loc. cit.*
[36] *Loc. cit.*
[37] *Loc. cit.*
[38] *Loc. cit.*

Nature is an effect of its cause, God. Hence an act against the effect is an act against the cause.[39]

But, having shown that laws must oblige in conscience, Soto still has to determine what the foundation of obligation is. Is it the will of the lawgiver or the very nature of the law itself? As mentioned, Soto saw difficulties in either alternative.[40] But they were not insoluble, if one seeks the solution in the objective nature of the acts commanded by the law.

So first, Soto says, a distinction must be made between ecclesiastical and civil authority. In making this distinction, Soto like Cajetan sets himself in contrast to those who have persisted in identifying the two. For, he says, those in ecclesiastical authority are judges of spiritual things and can make laws which not only constitute an act in a certain species of virtue or vice, but which also determine whether the transgression is a mortal or a venial sin. Those in civil authority, however, "cannot determine whether their laws will oblige under mortal or venial sin." It is the "nature itself of the acts" involved which will determine this most important point. If the matter of the act is grave, then the trangression will also be a matter of grave sin. By the making of the law the act specified is constituted a matter of obedience. Hence, if the matter of the law is of great consequence, its transgression is grave disobedience.[41]

Secondly, on account of the principle just laid down (that the gravity of the obligation is determined, not by the will of the lawgiver, but by the very nature of the acts in-

[39] *Ibid.*, q.4, a.2, p. 28.
[40] Cf. above, p. 169.
[41] *Ibid.*, q.6, a.4, p. 49.

volved), it is not necessary that the lawgiver even mention in the law whether it obliges under pain of mortal or venial sin. That can be determined by an examination of the nature of the act itself.[42]

Hence a trustworthy rule to follow is: Every law which is promulgated without any qualification obliges under pain of mortal or venial sin according to the nature of the act in question. The reason, Soto says, is evident. For law implies a command of obedience; and obedience is a virtue, disobedience is sin.[43] Therefore the ultimate reason why laws oblige, for Soto, is because their command is a matter of obedience.

If Soto had only asked himself, at this point, why obedience is a virtue, he would have had an opportunity to complete his application of the principle of finality based on the nature of things. For, as St. Thomas says, to obey is to be moved and be directed by the command of authority. But to command others is to move and direct them to their proper end. Therefore to obey is to be moved and directed to an end. Hence one is obliged to obey authority because it ordains means that are necessary for an end.[44]

Purely penal law? Soto's position in regard to purely penal civil law is based upon one fact: there can be no punishment if it is not on account of a preceding fault. Where there is no *culpa* there can be no true *poena*. By a true punishment is meant a rectification of a fault committed.[45]

[42] *Ibid.,* p. 50.
[43] *Loc. cit.*
[44] Cf. St. Thomas, *Sum. theol.,* II–II, q. 104, a. 1, c; *ibid.,* q. 102, a. 2, c.
[45] *Ibid.,* a. 5, p. 52.

Hence it can be taken as an infallible rule that no such severe punishment as death or mutilation can ever be inflicted except for a grave fault.[46] Soto concludes, therefore, that the concept of a law which obliges to the penalty and not to the fault is unintelligible. For "punishment of its very nature is the genuine effect and judgment of fault." Those who attempt to hold the opposite "have not philosophized on the nature of punishment." [47] For Soto, then, the concept of purely penal civil law is impossible. Laws oblige in conscience whether they carry the threat of a penalty or not.[48]

Hence Soto "sees no value in the distinction" between the so-called mixed laws and purely penal laws,[49] which distinction he says was given great impetus by Henry of Ghent.[50] As far as Soto is concerned, "there can be no penalty without a preceding fault." [51] Therefore there can be no law which does not oblige to what is specified. Consequently for Soto there can be no purely penal law.

But it is at this point that Soto introduces an idea that is somewhat surprising. He says that when punishment is applied to a fault, as in the above-mentioned laws, the obligation is in conscience under pain of sin. However, when the law has the form of concession or dispensation, then the law does not oblige under pain of sin, and that which has the name of punishment is not that at all. It is

---

[46] *Ibid.*, p. 53.
[47] *Loc. cit.*
[48] *Loc. cit.*
[49] Cf. above, Henry of Ghent, chap. 1; Castro, chap. 5; Suarez, chap. 6.
[50] *Loc. cit.*
[51] *Loc. cit.*

rather of the nature of an agreed price to be paid for the concession of doing what is prohibited by the law.

For example, if a law were made that whoever transported grain out of the country would lose it or would pay a certain penalty, such a law would oblige in conscience to refrain from what was forbidden by the law. However, if the intention of the lawgiver was, not to stop the removal of grain, but by this means to collect money, then the law would not oblige in conscience. The subjoined condition of penalty would not be a punishment but the price of the concession: whoever wished to remove grain would have to contribute accordingly.[52] The thing to be noted is that in such cases "that which appears to be a penalty is rather a price or an agreement or *quid aliud.*" [53]

What is the value of this *lex concessoria* of Soto? [54] While it may seem an easy way to save purely penal laws by turning them into laws of concession, in doing so Soto has taken back with the left hand what he had so resolutely proffered with the right. He has contradicted a basic principle of law that he himself has set down; namely, that law, if it is to be just, must be concerned with what is somehow necessary for the common good. Now, either the prohibition of the removal of grain (to use his example) is necessary for the common good, or it is not. If it is, then the law forbidding it obliges in conscience under pain of mortal or venial sin according to the gravity of the situation. If it is not necessary, then it should not be made a matter of law. For, public authority should not be concerned with

[52] *Ibid.,* p. 54.
[53] *Loc. cit.*
[54] *Loc. cit.*

what is not necessary for the common good. If it is money
that is immediately needed and therefore necessary for
the common good, then laws levying taxes should be enacted, not "laws" granting concessions in regard to something not necessarily related to the common good.

Having rejected purely penal law, Soto realizes that it
may be objected that there are purely penal laws in religious orders, such as his own. In these unions a subject
may be obliged only to the penalty without having committed any fault. Soto's answer to this difficulty is well
worth noting. It is consistent with his basic principles of
law and obligation. He says, much like Cajetan, that the
so-called *poena* imposed in the religious union is "not
properly and legitimately a punishment." It is rather "an
agreement or a pact." It is something the subject obliges
himself to accept by his vow for his own individual perfection. However, Soto says, these *poenae* are not unsuit-
ably called punishments because they are imposed on
account of things forbidden.[55]

Since, then, in the religious union there is question of
no true *poena* or *culpa,* there can be no question of true
law. The so-called "laws" of religious orders are rather
rules to which one voluntarily subscribes.

In regard to certain practical cases which in some quarters are interpreted even today as matter of purely penal
civil law, Soto is quite consistent. He applies his principles
well and concludes that such as tax laws, for instance,
oblige in conscience. If there is doubt about their justness,
judgment does not pertain to the subjects but to those in

[55] *Loc. cit.*

authority, unless it is a case of the most manifest tyranny.[56]

Soto, consequently, on the basis of his principle of the relation of *poena* to *culpa* cannot be said to hold purely penal law. It is true that certain statements that he does make seem, on the surface, to suggest that he holds it.[57] But these certainly must be interpreted in the light of what he has said in regard to the fact that there can be no true *poena* without a preceding *culpa*. If the lawgiver says that it is his intention not to oblige in conscience, then, according to Soto's principles at least, the "law" in question must be either a rule of a religious union or an agreement in regard to a concession, neither of which is a true law.

Soto then, following St. Thomas, maintains the primacy of the intellect over the will. He holds that there is an act of the intellect after the election: the command. Hence the essence of the law is this act, the command of the intellect. With command thus established as an act of the intellect ordering and directing means necessary for an end, the foundation of obligation must be the objective relation of these means necessary for the end. Therefore there can be no true purely penal law.

But, like Cajetan, at times he left much to be desired in his explanation of certain points. In allowing no command before the election, he is on better ground than Cajetan

---

[56] *Ibid.*, IV, q.6, a.4, pp. 361 f.

[57] Thus, for instance, Soto says that "whoever, whether a secular or ecclesiastical ruler, wishes to make a law which would not oblige in conscience, should explain it" (*De just. et jure*, I, q.6, a.4). He also says that "there is absolutely no penal law, if it is properly named, which does not oblige in conscience, unless it expresses the contrary intention by saying 'We do not intend to oblige in conscience,' or something similar" (*ibid.*, a.5).

and is closer to St. Thomas, though in doing so he fails to save the intellectual element of the election. But in limiting prudence to something which follows an election of specification and not seeing in prudence an election of exercise, Soto made a fatal error from which he was not able to free himself. No one was more aware of this fact than his adversaries.

CHAPTER XI

BARTHOLOMEW MEDINA

I

BARTHOLOMEW MEDINA, O.P. (1528–80), was a very zealous and personal commentator on St. Thomas. He taught after Soto at Salamanca, holding the chair of theology from 1576 to 1580, and took strict issue with him on his interpretation of parts of St. Thomas' psychology. Though Medina's interpretation tended to be intellectualistic to the extreme,—to be noted is his strong opposition to Scotus—his perception of the relation between psychology and the nature of law is clearer and better thought out than Soto's.[1]

Intellect superior. The intellect is the superior faculty. Although the will may be said to be superior inasmuch as it is the principle of motion, yet, absolutely speaking, the intellect is superior inasmuch as it is the principle of knowledge and direction.[2] As Aristotle had said, the in-

---

[1] A good account of the life, works, and importance of Medina may be found in Gorce's article, "Medina," *Dictionnaire de théologie catholique,* X (1928), 482–85. Cf. also Hurter, *Nomenclator* (2nd ed., 1892), p. 45; Quetif-Echard, *Scriptores ordinis praedicatorum* (Paris, 1719), II, 256 f.

He is not to be confused with John Medina (1490–1547), who wrote *De poenitentia, restitutione et contractibus* (Ingolstadt, 1581).

[2] *Expositio in primam secundae angelici doctoris D. Thomae Aquinatis,* q. 17, a. 1, sol., p. 253.

tellect is the most excellent power of the soul.[3] If the will is the queen, Medina adds, then the intellect is the king and emperor. For the intellect rules the will and prescribes a rule of action for it, without which both would fall into the pit. All right thinking men, Medina says, have always held that prudence commands and that the will should obey. "Only the most perverted" hold the opposite, saying: *Sic volo, sic iubeo, sit pro ratione voluntas.*[4]

Command: act of the intellect. The act of command, then, could be for Medina only an act of the intellect.[5] Why? First, because the command is an act of speaking or intimation. Such an act, however, is the work of the intellect. Secondly, to command is to rule and govern. But this also is an act of the intellect. Hence the command is an act of the intellect.[6] It is principally, then, because the command is an act of direction of means to an end, which implies intellectual perception, that it is an act of the intellect.[7]

Scotus, Medina says, admitted the command, but referred it to the will. He spoke "most obscurely," however, on this matter.[8] All other philosophers, notes Medina, agree with Aristotle that the will obeys reason.[9]

If it should be objected that the command cannot be an act of the intellect because the acts of the intellect are either

---

3 *Ibid.,* expl., p. 252.
4 *Ibid.,* ad 4, p. 252.
5 *Ibid.,* concl., p. 251.
6 *Ibid.,* p. 252.
7 *Ibid.,* ad 3, p. 252. Cf. *ibid.,* sol., p. 253.
8 *Ibid.,* p. 251.
9 *Ibid.,* p. 252.

apprehensive or judicative and the command is neither, Medina answers: There are many acts of the intellect which are neither apprehensive nor judicative. Prayer or promise, for instance, are of this nature. Hence the command may be said to be "reduced to a judgment, for it is something like a conclusion and the last part of a judgment." [10]

If the command is an act of the intellect, it must follow from a habit of the intellect. Command, then, is the principal act of the intellectual habit of prudence.[11] So, just as one commands his own body with what may be called a servile command and his sense appetite with a political or civil command, so also the one in authority commands his subjects.[12]

Medina, like St. Thomas, has said that the command is an act of the intellect, but presupposing an act of the will. So the question arises: What, for Medina, is the relation between the intellect and will and what is their interaction?

The election pertains to both the intellect and the will. As Aristotle said, it is an act either of the intellective appetite or of the appetitive intellect.[13]

The origin of liberty is to be found, however, in the indetermination and indifference of the intellect.[14] But the act of election is itself, of course, elicited by the will.[15] Hence "the election is substantially an act of the will."

10 *Ibid.*, ad 2, p. 252.
11 *Ibid.*, p. 253. Cf. *ibid.*, p. 251.
12 *Ibid.*, p. 252.
13 *Ibid.*, q. 13, a. 1, c. 1, p. 224.
14 *Ibid.*, q. 1, a. 1, p. 2.
15 *Ibid.*, q. 5, a. 2, c. 1, p. 127.

And, says Medina following St. Thomas, because the substance of an act is as matter to the order imposed by a
higher power,[16] "the election is materially of the will and
formally of the intellect." [17] Therefore the determining
factor in the interaction of the intellect and will is that,
although the will may be the source of motion, only the
intellect is the principle of order and direction.[18]

But what is the relation between the election and the
command? Medina, like Cajetan, says the command may
be taken in two ways. First, it may be taken as that act of
prudence which precedes the election and commands the
will to elect here and now, this or that. Secondly, the command may be taken to denote the act which follows the
election and applies the powers of the soul to action.[19]

Now Soto, as Medina says, "vehemently" denied that
there could be such an act of command before the election.[20] Hence Medina attempts to show why Soto was
wrong and why there must be a command before the
election. He says that the act of prudence precedes the
election, because the election needs direction. But the act
of prudence is the command which directs. Therefore
command precedes the election. Prudence is the directrix
of all virtues. Hence there can be no act of a virtue without
the act of prudence. But the election is an act of a virtue,
and the command is the act of prudence. Therefore the
command precedes the election.[21]

16 *Ibid.*, q. 13, a. 1, c. 3, p. 225. Cf. *ibid.*, n., p. 225.
17 *Ibid.*, c. 2, p. 224.
18 *Ibid.*, sol., p. 226.
19 *Ibid.*, q. 17, a. 3, p. 254.
20 *Loc. cit.* Cf. above, Soto, chap. 10.
21 *Loc. cit.*

Does this mean that, once the command is given on the part of the intellect, the election necessarily follows? Yes, answers Medina, "the election necessarily and infallibly follows." Nor does this mean, he adds, that no habit is necessary for disposing the will to the election, or that the election is not meritorious and praiseworthy. For although the election necessarily follows the command of the intellect, "since this is a conditional necessity and one following from a supposition, human liberty remains intact." [22]

How does this take place? How does the intellect command the will so that it necessarily elects according to the command without losing its liberty? What kind of causality does the intellect exercise here: is it final, formal, or efficient causality?

Though Medina is willing to admit that final or formal causality is here possible,[23] he says that what seems probable to him is "that the intellect by the command moves the will with efficient causality." [24]

In explanation of this position Medina says that first, when seeking how the intellect moves the will, we must keep in mind that there is no question here of the speculative intellect, but only of the practical intellect. For the speculative intellect moves nothing, but the practical intellect always moves the will efficiently.

How does this take place? It occurs through prudence, the habit of the practical intellect. Prudence "by its command, efficaciously lays hold (*rapit*) of the will and its habits." For, "once the intellect commands efficaciously,

22 *Loc. cit.*
23 *Ibid.*, q.9, a.1, p. 166.
24 *Ibid.*, c.2, p. 167.

there is no liberty left in the will to oppose it. This is a most evident sign that the command of the intellect efficaciously seizes the will." [25]

If it should be objected that the command of prudence has its efficacy to move from the will itself, for prudence is a moral virtue which in its operation depends on the will, Medina is ready with his answer. For, he says, although it is true that the command is sometimes efficacious from the volition which moves the intellect to command, nevertheless, since there cannot be process *in infinitum,* you must come to one command of the intellect which precedes all action of the will and which of itself efficaciously necessitates and controls the will.[26]

But what of the fact that whenever Aristotle and St. Thomas spoke of the intellect moving the will it was by means of final causality: not as though the intellect actually inclines the will to that to which it tends, but as showing it that to which it should tend? [27] Medina answers by saying that, even when the apprehended good is taken as in the intention, and not metaphorically, it has conjoined with it the efficacious command of the intellect that efficaciously controls the will.[28]

However, it still may be objected that the will is the principal cause of volition. Hence, if the apprehended good concurs effectively in volition, it must do so either as form

[25] *Loc. cit.*

[26] *Loc. cit.* It is interesting to note that Medina uses *imperium* as well as *praeceptum* to denote the command of prudence. Cf. above, St. Thomas, chap. 8.

[27] *Ibid.,* q.9, a.1, p. 166. Medina seems not to have taken cognizance of the fact that St. Thomas in his later writings on this subject spoke less of final and more of formal causality. Cf. above, chap. 8.

[28] *Ibid.,* ad 1, p. 167.

or as an instrument. But it cannot concur as form because the form should be conjoined with the act itself, and the good apprehended is in another power. Nor can it concur as an instrument because an instrument is moved by a principal agent, and the apprehended good is not moved by the will.[29]

Medina's answer to this difficulty is revealing. For it shows how he interpreted St. Thomas' explanation of the material and formal causal interaction of the intellect and will in their composite acts. He says that the apprehended good does concur as a form by the mediation of which the will produces its actions. But "the form does not have to be conjoined to the act itself. It is sufficient that it be in the same essence of the soul." For, Medina adds, it is proper to the will to act through the good apprehended by another power of the same soul.[30]

From this it can only be concluded that Medina misunderstood the interaction of the intellect and will as explained by St. Thomas. He seems not to have grasped the meaning and importance of material and formal causality in the composite act. And therefore he completely separated the election from prudence. The election did not belong to prudence. It was that which prudence commanded. He seems to have entirely overlooked those places in St. Thomas where the Angelic Doctor speaks of prudence as the *habitus electivus*.[31] If prudence is not the habit

29 *Loc. cit.*
30 *Ibid.*, ad 5, p. 167.
31 Cf., for instance, St. Thomas, *De virt. in comm.*, q. un., a. 12 ad 26; *Sum. theol.*, I–II, q. 57, a. 5.

which rightly disposes to the decision to act, then what habit is?

Once a command is placed before the election, as an act entirely separate from it, it is hard to see how liberty is preserved. Suarez was right when he referred to this very passage we have been discussing, as an example of a doctrine that destroyed liberty.[32]

Even Medina's successor, Bañez (1528–1604), saw that Medina's position was too severe and led to the destruction of liberty.[33] In fact, he well notes the similarity between Medina's doctrine and Cajetan's, both of whom held that the intellect could effectively move the will. The only difference, he says, was that Medina put the whole efficacy of moving the will in the command; whereas Cajetan attributed this force to the object inasmuch as it is under the practical apprehension.[34]

Bañez, it is worth noting, in a most lucid passage gives the liberating word to the whole discussion when he says that "the will seeks the perfection of the intellect more than its own." For there is no question here, he says, of two supposits, but of two powers ordered to the perfection of one supposit. And "since *ipsum intelligere* is that which is most fitting to man because his form is intellectual, it is to it that the will is most inclined: to *ipsum intelligere*." [35]

[32] Suarez, *Disp. metaph.*, XIX, c.6, n.2. Cf. above also, Suarez, chap. 6.

[33] Domingo Bañez, O.P., *Comentarios ineditos a la Prima Secundae de Santo Tomas* (Madrid, 1942), q.9, a.1. An account of Bañez' works and importance may be found in *Kirchenlexicon*, I (2nd ed.), 1948–65. Cf. also Mandonnet, "Bañez," *Dictionnaire de théologie catholique*, II (1932), 139–45.

[34] *Loc. cit.*

[35] *Ibid.*, q.3, a.4.

Bañez has much to offer by way of clarification of this most abstruse subject of the causal relation of the intellect and will.[36]

Medina, then, although his explanation of it is faulty, holds that the command is an act of the intellect. What he will hold in regard to the nature of law is, consequently, already indicated.

II

Law: act of the intellect. For Medina, law is the command. But the command is, as he has said, an act of the intellect. Therefore law is an act of the intellect.[37] Then too, law is a rule which directs the will. But direction pertains only to the intellect. Hence law is of the intellect.[38]

Without this direction of the command of law, no home, no city, no people would be possible. In fact, the whole human race, the very nature of things, and even the world itself depends upon it.[39]

Another reason why law is of the intellect is that in the will there is only volition and nolition. In the will there is no command. For, although I know that the superior wishes, for instance, that I read, I am not obliged to obey until he speaks to me and commands me. But to speak and command pertain to the intellect. Therefore law is not of the will, but of the intellect.[40]

Law, then, which is essentially the command that di-

---

[36] Cf. especially his comment on I–II, q.9, a.1 (*op. cit.*). Bañez was not fully treated here because not enough of his works are available.

[37] Medina, *op. cit.*, q.90, a.1, p. 822.

[38] *Loc. cit.*

[39] *Ibid.*, p. 823.

[40] *Loc. cit.*

rects means to an end, is an act of the practical, not the speculative, intellect.[41] It includes the will, but only inasmuch as the will approves what the intellect has previously judged to be good. Then the command follows.[42]

Medina, by his explanation of prudence commanding the election, has already made a truly composite act of intellect and will impossible. However, he continues to speak as if he were still dealing with one. For he says that when two powers concur to produce one act, to that power must the act be attributed substantially in which it is found most perfectly. Now, law is substantially command, rule, and light. And since these pertain only to the intellect, so law is of the intellect substantially.[43] Consequently, when law is said to be the will of the legislator,—for instance, in Scripture it is called "the will of God"—this means only that the force of directing comes from the will of the legislator, not the direction itself.[44]

If the intellect directs means to an end, then the principle of direction must be the end itself. Hence all laws must be directed to the attainment of the common good.[45] This principle of finality is, in fact, that according to which good government is distinguished from tyranny.[46]

Medina, recognizing the importance of order and finality in the concept of law, interprets accordingly the analogous nature of law, from the eternal to the most particular temporal law.

[41] *Loc. cit.*
[42] *Loc. cit.*
[43] *Ibid.*, n., p. 823.
[44] *Ibid.*, ad 1, p. 824.
[45] *Ibid.*, q.90, a.2, p. 824.
[46] *Ibid.*, p. 826.

Since law is the dictate of practical reason governing a community, the divine intellect is the eternal law governing the world.[47] The eternal law is then, not the divine will, as Scotus would have it,[48] but the divine intellect directing everything to its end.[49] Once having so well stated this principle of finality, Medina easily shows how it is verified in all the analogues of law. For, says Medina paraphrasing St. Thomas, all created things participate by their very form and inclinations in the divine ordering to an end. And so far as this is true, they are by participation law, natural law.[50] Human law is only a determination of the natural law.[51] Hence it also participates in the ordering to an end, and is truly law.[52] The analogy of law, then, based on the principle of ordination of means to an end, finds good expression in Medina.

Obligation: from the relation of means to the end. But if law is essentially an ordering of means to an end, is this also the reason why laws oblige?

Medina is explicit, even emphatic, in saying that it is not the will of the lawgiver that is the source of obligation. On the contrary, if the lawgiver makes a law and "does not even think of obliging" his subjects, the subjects are nevertheless obliged to obey the law. For, "from the very making of the law itself, obligation necessarily follows." [53] A more

---

47 *Ibid.*, q.91, a.1, p. 835.
48 Cf. above, Scotus, chap. 2.
49 *Ibid.*, q.93, a.1, p. 849.
50 *Ibid.*, q.91, a.2, p. 835.
51 *Ibid.*, q.95, a.2, p. 871.
52 *Ibid.*, pp. 870 f.
53 *Ibid.*, q.90, a.1, n., p. 823.

forthright statement of the objective foundation of obligation could scarcely be wished.

But what is the exact reason why obligation must necessarily follow from the very making of a law? Medina gives two reasons, one too general to be satisfying, the other specific and clearly establishing the foundation of obligation in the necessary relation of the means commanded by law to the end, the common good.

First, he says, human law is from God. Therefore it obliges in conscience as well as the divine law does. For human legislators, by delegated divine authority, can oblige as God does.[54] True though this may be, it still leaves the question unanswered: How do human legislators participate in divine authority? So Medina says that, secondly, obligation follows from law because unless it does, the end for which laws command means cannot be attained. Civil and ecclesiastical authority is necessary to attain the respective ends of the civil and ecclesiastical unions, namely, public peace and the supernatural end. But this authority is meaningless unless the laws oblige in conscience.[55] Therefore they oblige because of the relation of that which laws command to the common good.[56]

Hence, because human law is a participation in the divine directing and ordering of all things to an end, human authority, which establishes a like ordering, participates in the divine authority. And because one is obliged to obey divine law, since what it commands is necessary for the

54 *Ibid.*, q.96, a.4, p. 876.
55 *Ibid.*, pp. 876 f.
56 *Ibid.*, soi., p. 877.

end, so one is obliged to obey human law for the same reason: what it commands is necessary to obtain an end. It is the objective relation of means commanded by law to the common good, that is the foundation of obligation.

The stress that Medina lays on the importance of the objective nature of acts and their necessary relation to an end is further shown by his explanation of the difference between the obligation under pain of mortal and venial sin. To say, Medina states, that the force of obliging under pain of mortal or venial sin depends on the will of the lawgiver is false. For "if the legislator seriously and truly commands something otherwise grave and greatly contributive to the common good, it is not in his power to determine whether or not it obliges under pain of mortal sin." Again, "if the legislator commands something otherwise not grave and of small moment, it is not in his power to determine that the law oblige under pain of mortal sin." [57]

Hence the first rule to be followed, Medina says, in determining whether a law obliges under pain of mortal or venial sin is: Examine the matter. If the matter is grave and greatly conducive to the common good, then the law obliges under pain of mortal sin; otherwise not. The second rule is: When the transgression is against charity or justice, the law obliges under pain of mortal sin; otherwise under pain of venial sin. The third rule is: When the law threatens capital punishment or perpetual exile, it obliges under pain of mortal sin. The severity of the penalty is an argument that the thing commanded is grave.

[57] *Ibid.*, pp. 877 f.

The fourth rule: When the law commands something under the sentence of anathema, this is evidence that it obliges under pain of mortal sin. The fifth rule: To transgress a human law out of contempt is a mortal sin. For to contemn the superior is a mortal sin. This rule, however, Medina admits, is not too certain. For to contemn a law within the limits of a law that is not in regard to grave matter is only a venial sin.[58]

Purely penal law? Granting, now, that all laws oblige in conscience, do they necessarily oblige to what is commanded, or only to the payment of the penalty? In other words, is purely penal civil law possible?

Medina is most emphatic in rejecting the notion of purely penal civil law. For, he says, it is an inseparable property of law that it oblige in conscience to what is commanded, as has been shown. But penal laws are true laws. Therefore they oblige in conscience to what is commanded.[59] Henry of Ghent's distinction is therefore to be rejected.[60] For, Medina repeats, all laws with a penalty attached oblige in conscience to that which is commanded. Punishment has no meaning except in relation to fault previously committed. Why? Because, Medina explains, it was through fault that punishment had its origin. On account of the sin of one man, death entered into the world. Then too, punishment is the medicine of fault. What is injured by fault is restored by punishment.[61]

58 *Ibid.*, p. 878.
59 *Ibid.*, p. 880.
60 *Loc. cit.*
61 *Loc. cit.*

Therefore Medina concludes, first, that punishment should correspond to the fault committed. Hence the very fact that the legislator inflicts a punishment on transgressors shows that he wishes to oblige in conscience. Secondly, if the legislator makes laws without any punishment attached, all admit that they oblige in conscience. Therefore, if he attaches a punishment, evidently the laws also oblige in conscience. For, the attaching of a punishment is only a sign of how much more ardently the legislator wishes his command to be obeyed. Thirdly, legislators attach different degrees of punishment on transgressors. But this shows they consider that different degrees of fault have been committed. Fourthly, when legislators command something under threat of punishment, they thereby constitute it under virtue and obedience. Hence the contrary is a vice. Finally, there can be no doubt about the fact that, if an officer commands a soldier, under threat of death, not to desert his post, and he deserts, it is a mortal sin. In fact it is a general rule that, whenever a law commands under pain of death or privation of all goods or perpetual exile, it obliges under mortal sin.[62]

The necessary relation between penalty and fault is therefore evident. There can be no law imposing a penalty which does not also oblige in conscience to what it commands. In other words, there can be no purely penal civil law.

But what about some laws that certainly do not oblige in conscience to what is commanded but only to the payment of the penalty (as, for instance, the law that forbids cutting

[62] *Ibid.*, p. 880.

wood in the public forest).[63] Medina's answer is consistent with his principles. Such "laws" are not true laws. They are at most "agreements of the people themselves" freely entered into lest the public forest be destroyed. Or, he says, such "laws" are "statutes with a disjunction: If anyone cuts wood, he will pay a certain penalty." [64] Though all this is quite reasonable, Medina seems to have overlooked one possibility. If the public forest is so important that it is necessary for the common good and should be preserved, then it is legitimate matter for a true law obliging in conscience, even if a penalty is attached.

Finally, the rejection of purely penal law seems overruled, Medina says, by the fact that there actually are such laws—in religious orders.[65] Medina's answer is the same as above, and with justification. He says that "the constitutions of religious unions, which do not oblige in conscience under pain of sin, are not true laws. Nor does the superior in such unions, strictly speaking, command or demand obedience. These constitutions are more of the nature of admonitions and counsels than laws. For it is the property of law that it oblige in conscience under pain of sin. If it is a law, it is a matter of obedience. To depart from it, then, is wrong and a sin." [66] Hence, for Medina, the rules of religious orders are not laws, for they do not oblige under sin. It is a misnomer to call them purely penal "laws." Therefore the existence of religious rules does not constitute an argument in favor of purely penal law.

63 *Ibid.*, p. 880.
64 *Ibid.*, ad 3, p. 881.
65 *Ibid.*, p. 878.
66 *Loc. cit.*

Therefore Medina, because in his psychology he holds that the command is an act of the intellect, also holds that law is of the intellect. And because he recognizes the part that objective essences must play as a basis of morality, he also recognizes that the foundation of obligation is the objective relation of means to an end. True, his explanation of the relation between prudence and the election is faulty. It was rejected by his pupils, and his opponents took it as a prime example of where the principles of so-called "Thomism" could lead. Medina's instincts were right regarding where he should go. But he was not wholly successful in finding the way that led there.

CHAPTER XII

ROBERT BELLARMINE

I

St. Robert Bellarmine, S.J. (1542–1621), taught theology at the Jesuit College at Louvain from 1570 to 1576. For his text he replaced the *Sentences* of Lombard with the *Summa theologiae* of St. Thomas. It was not until twenty-six years later that the university itself instituted the *Summa* as the text.

Bellarmine's great preoccupation was, of course, with stemming the tide of religious revolt. Hence his *Controversies* are considered his main work. It was during the course of these labors that he was confronted with the reformers' loose notion of law which was based on a primacy of the will. Reacting against such an idea of law and its foundation in the will, Bellarmine put forward St. Thomas' concept of law as based on the primacy of the intellect. Whether his part in this great religious struggle had anything to do with it, Bellarmine's mind seems to have been sharpened to a finer appreciation of St. Thomas' psychology and his philosophy of law than were the minds of some of his own confreres.

Since Bellarmine's commentary on the *Summa* of Aquinas has not yet been published,[1] we shall have to find his philosophy of intellect and will and his concept of law in the *Controversies*. It is remarkable that even though the prime purpose of these writings is not philosophical, as their title indicates, Bellarmine's fine grasp of St. Thomas' principles ever continues to shine through.

Intellect: the superior faculty. For Bellarmine the intellect is the superior faculty. The will being the inferior power must always obey the intellect, the superior power.[2] As a matter of fact, although the will is formally free, the root of this liberty is in reason. For the will is free because it is a rational appetite, just as on the contrary the appetite in brutes is not free because it is not rational. Therefore the cause of liberty is reason itself.[3]

Besides, the appetite cannot be inclined to something unless this is proposed by a power which knows it as good and perfective. Nor can the appetite withdraw from an object unless it is proposed to it as evil and harmful.

---

[1] It is most unfortunate and lamentable that his first four volumes of commentary on the *Summa* are unpublished and therefore unavailable. The publication of this work would only be making known a man who more than deserves to be established in his rightful place in the line of Thomistic commentators.

The manuscript at present is at the Gregorian University in Rome and is being prepared for publication by a member of the staff of that university. Early appearance, however, of the work is not promised.

[2] *Disputationes Roberti Bellarmini de controversiis christianae fidei adversus huius temporis haereticos: De amiss. grat. et stat. pecc.*, V, c.14, 322E–323A. One of the best general accounts of Bellarmine's life and works is J. Brodrick, S.J., *The Life and Work of Blessed Robert Francis Cardinal Bellarmine, S.J.* (London: Burns Oates and Washbourne, 1928). Cf. also Le Bachelet, "Bellarmine," *Dictionnaire de théologie catholique*, II (1932), 560–99; *Kirchenlexicon*, II (1883), 285–93; E. Ryan, S.J., *The Historical Scholarship of St. Bellarmine* (New York: Fordham University Press, 1936).

[3] *De gratia et lib. arbit.*, III, c.8, 497E.

Hence, if the power which knows is determined to one thing, that is, if it proposes only one thing, whether good or bad, the appetite necessarily tends to it or withdraws from it. This we see take place even in brutes, whose knowledge is sensible and consequently determined to one thing. But if the power which knows is undetermined and proposes various objects,—showing that in each there are aspects of good and bad, and then opening up the way to their opposites, for such is the nature of our own reason in regard to means that are not necessarily connected with an end—then the appetite will be free and will be able to be inclined to various objects. Hence the will is free because it follows reason, which proposes various and contingent means of obtaining an end.[4]

Bellarmine staunchly takes his stand against those who, like Henry of Ghent and Scotus, say that the will is in no way determined by the intellect; that reason cannot be free formally because the intellect, if we prescind from ignorance and error, necessarily judges that a thing is; that reason is not free radically because the word "root" signifies a true cause; that reason instead of being the cause of liberty is only a condition without which there would be no liberty in the will.[5] Rather, says Bellarmine, the doctrine of St. Thomas seems to him most true: that the root of liberty is in reason and that the will depends upon and is determined by the last judgment of practical reason.

What is this last judgment of practical reason? Is it the command preceding the election, as Cajetan and Medina

---

[4] *Ibid.*, 497E–498A.
[5] *Ibid.*, c.7, 493C-D.

held? Is it the judgment of *synesis* with only an indirect relation to the election through a disposition, as Soto held? Or is it the judged election, elected judgment of St. Thomas?

To his everlasting credit let it be said that for Bellarmine it was the last: it was the judged election, elected judgment. For this reason, if for no other, he is immediately set off and distinguished from the previous commentators on St. Thomas whom we have been considering.

For, he says, "by the name of election he understands, not precisely the act of the will that follows the last judgment, but that act together with the conclusion of the last judgment itself." Therefore in the act of election Bellarmine maintains the intellectual as well as the volitional elements, the basis of St. Thomas' material and formal causality of this composite act. Aristotle, Bellarmine says, had said the same thing: that the election was consultative appetition; that it was intellective appetition or appetitive election. Aristotle also said that the election was a sort of conclusion of the practical syllogism because "the conclusion of the last practical judgment and the act of the will are taken as one and the same thing." And Gregory of Nyssa had said that the election was something composed of counsel and appetite. Finally, Bellarmine adds, St. Thomas himself says that, though the election is an act elicited by the will, it also includes an act of the intellect. Hence "the election or choice—embracing as it does both acts, namely, the last judgment of the intellect and the approbation of the will—is truly in regard to many things and is therefore completely in our power and absolutely free." [6]

Bellarmine therefore did not keep the action of the intellect separated from the action of the will in the composite act of election. He realized too well (as Bañez did) [7] that intellect and will were only two powers working for the perfection of the whole supposit. For, he says, the will does not move the reason or the other powers as if by impressing something upon them. But it may be said to move them actively, because "the will is a kind of impulse of the whole supposit toward the accomplishment of the acts of all the powers. So man himself, because by his will he desires to know the truth, moves himself to exercise intelligence. The same is true of the other powers. Nor can it be said, on the other hand, that the will is moved in the same way by the intellect. It cannot be said that man, because he knows the good through reason, impels himself to that good so that it may be loved by the will. For reason or intelligence is not an impulse or inclination, but rather a susception or apprehension. The will, on the other hand, is by its very nature an inclination and an impulse, not only of itself but also . . . of the whole supposit." [8]

It is in the light of these expressions of his fundamental position, then, that we must understand all Bellarmine's subsequent statements in regard to this problem.

Hence the election of the will depends necessarily, in the sense explained, on the last judgment of practical

[6] *Ibid.*, c. 10, 501E–502A.
[7] Cf. above, chap. 11.
[8] *Ibid.*, 504C.

reason. For, the object of the will is the good apprehended and judged to be perfective. For this reason, if the will should wish something without this preceding knowledge and judgment, it would be acting without an object—which cannot happen.[9] For if, Bellarmine explains, when there is a judgment completely determined to one object, the will could choose another object or not choose this one; then no reason could be given why the will would choose the other object not judged, or why it would not choose this one already judged. So, there would be an election without a judgment, and action without an object—which is impossible.[10]

The will "is free in electing, not because it is not necessarily determined by the last and practical judgment of reason, but because this ultimate and practical judgment is in the power of the will," [11] as explained. For, Bellarmine further states, after there is knowledge of the good in general, there exists in the will an inclination to it, but not a complete election. Various means are proposed by reason, showing the good and bad in each. The will is inclined now one way, now another. But it is in its power to allow itself to be moved, or it may resist. This is not done by any positive act but by a negative one, by not permitting itself to be moved. "By the very fact that the will permits itself to be moved by one of the proposed means, the mind, omitting all other inquiry, proceeds, and concludes a particular judgment, which is immediately followed by the election. Hence the liberty of the will seems

9 *Ibid.*, c.8, 496C-D.
10 *Ibid.*, 496E.
11 *Ibid.*, c.9, 500A.

to consist properly in this: that the will may allow itself
to be moved by one thing and not by another." [12] When
Bellarmine says that the particular judgment is "immediately followed by the election," we should remember
that this is to be taken as the act of election *"together with
the conclusion of the last judgment itself."* [13] Hence for
Bellarmine the act of the intellect that is directly and causally related to the election is neither the command of prudence as Cajetan and Medina held nor the judgment of
synesis as Soto thought, but the judgment of election.

Command: act of the intellect. What then did Bellarmine hold in regard to the command? Did he hold that
it was an act of the intellect as was held by St. Thomas,
whose *Summa theologiae* he was teaching?

There is no doubt that Bellarmine held that the command is an act of the intellect. For, as already noted, it is
the intellect, according to Bellarmine, that commands and
directs the will: [14] not in regard to electing, as is shown in
the passage given above, but in regard to executing the
means that will lead to the end.

When speaking of law, as we shall see, he says that law,
which is of reason, commands the will of the subject.
Hence command is of the intellect.[15] The command
obliges because it is concerned with means to an end,
which, according to the principles of intellect and will Bellarmine has already established, is a relation that could per-

12 *Ibid.*, 500A-B. Cf. *ibid.*, IV, c.16, 556D.
13 Cf. above, p. 198 (italics added).
14 *De amiss. grat. et stat. pecc.*, V, c.14, 322E–323A.
15 *Ibid.*, 322E.

tain only to the intellect.[16] And as Bellarmine has rejected the philosophy of intellect and will of those who hold that command is of the will (such as Henry of Ghent and Scotus), no other alternative would be left to him if he is to be consistent.

For a fuller treatment of Bellarmine's position on the command, however, we shall have to wait for the publication of his above-mentioned commentary on the *Summa theologiae* of St. Thomas.[17]

II

Law: act of the intellect. Bellarmine's concept of law is expressed in terms all of which denote an act of the intellect. Law, he says, is a command and a rule.[18] It is a rule directing actions.[19] It is an ordering to a certain end, and hence it is an act of the intellect.[20]

So, in order that a law may be just, the four conditions, based on the four causes, laid down by St. Thomas must be verified.[21] Of special importance is the condition based on final cause: that the law must be for the common good. This is the very *raison d'être* of both civil and ecclesiastical law.[22] In fact, it is because subjects need direction, according to reason, to the end that laws are necessary, both civil and ecclesiastical.[23]

---

16 *Ibid.,* c. 10, 299B.
17 Cf. above, note 1.
18 *De laicis,* III, c. 10, 469C. Cf. *De amiss. grat. et stat. pecc.,* V, c. 10, 301D.
19 *De gratia et lib. arbit.,* V, c. 14, 601B. Cf. *De laicis,* III, c. 11, 471D, 473D.
20 *De clericis,* I, c. 29, 302B.
21 *De romano pont.,* IV, c. 15, 845C.
22 *De matrimonii sacramento,* I, c. 21, 1281C.
23 *De romano pont.,* IV, c. 16, 856A.

The intellectual nature of law is further brought out by Bellarmine's placing the eternal law in the divine intellect, which is the most perfect rule and therefore directs. All other law is but a participation in this directing and regulating. For, explains Bellarmine, all law—whether natural or positive, and positive both of God and of man—is law because it corresponds with the eternal law, which is the highest reason itself in God and the most perfect rule. Every true law is nothing but an adumbration and a participation in the eternal law.[24]

In God, His very wisdom is a law unto Himself. "What is law to us is nature to God." [25] Bellarmine will have none of the supremacy of the divine will. If, he says, God would impel men to do something contrary to the eternal law, and therefore to His nature and wisdom, such as adultery, then His will would be evil because it would be in opposition to the right rule of divine wisdom. Thus would God be contradicting Himself—which is impossible.[26] On the contrary, the divine will, by the very nature of God Himself, is always conformed to His divine wisdom.[27]

The full implications of law, as an act of the intellect directing means necessary for an end, are summed up by Bellarmine when he says: To recede from the rule of the eternal law, which is the divine wisdom, is a sin. This, of course, is impossible on God's part, for to recede from the

[24] *De amiss. grat. et stat. pecc.*, I, c. 1, 59B.
[25] *Ibid.*, II, c.4, 108E.
[26] *Loc. cit.* Cf. above, Ockham, chap. 3, and Biel, chap. 4, for the opposite opinion.
[27] *Ibid.*, 108E–109A.

divine wisdom would be to recede from Himself since He is divine wisdom itself. But for man to do this is to turn away from his final end and his greatest good, which is God. And this is a sin.[28]

The importance of finality is further manifested in Bellarmine's thought by his basis for distinguishing between the civil and the ecclesiastical unions. They are to be distinguished, he says, principally on account of their ends. The end of the civil union, and hence of civil authority, is "an external and temporal" one: the peace of the community. The end of the ecclesiastical union and ecclesiastical authority is, on the contrary, something "internal and eternal": the supernatural life of each individual.[29] In other words, if union takes its formal aspect from the end on account of which it exists, then these are, strictly speaking, different types of union. For the end of one is something that is *common* to all; while the end of the other is uniquely *proper* to each individual. Bellarmine will use this same principle later to distinguish the rules of the religious union from the laws of a civil union.[30]

Obligation: from the nature of the act. Bellarmine has clearly enough established law as an act of the intellect directing means to the common good. But how does he show that laws oblige?

The question of whether human laws oblige was a much mooted one during Bellarmine's time. Calvin said that civil laws did not oblige in conscience, which was

---

28 *Ibid.*, c. 10, 123D.
29 *De romano pont.*, IV, c. 21, 865D.
30 Cf. below, pp. 214 f.

what John Gerson had taught before him. Their reasons for holding this, Bellarmine says, were: first, political power, being only temporal, has nothing to do with conscience; secondly, the end of civil laws is external peace; thirdly, the lawgiver cannot judge about internal things; fourthly, the lawgiver cannot inflict a spiritual punishment, therefore neither can he oblige in conscience; fifthly, the lawgiver cannot absolve, therefore neither should he oblige; sixthly, the same sin would be punished twice, once in this world and once in the next; seventhly, the lawgiver does not ordinarily intend to oblige in conscience; eighthly, we should rather transgress a grave civil law than a slight divine law, as, for instance, the law not to lie officiously. But this law obliges only as a venial fault. Therefore the civil law does not oblige under pain of any fault. Because, if it did oblige under pain of fault or sin, especially mortal, then we should avoid mortal rather than venial sin.[31]

In this manner then, Bellarmine says, Luther and Calvin and others attempt to liberate the faithful from obedience to both divine and human laws, but in different ways. They affirm that divine laws oblige in conscience, so that it is a sin to violate them. But they add that such transgressions are either granted to the faithful or not imputed to them: which is, he says, the same as if they were entirely freed from the observance of these laws. In regard to human laws, whether ecclesiastical or political, these men also affirm, Bellarmine continues, that such laws do not oblige in conscience, unless it is by reason of scandal or

[31] *De laicis,* III, c.9, 469A-B.

contempt, which are prohibited by the divine law. And so, he concludes, to transgress a human law, even studiously, is not only not imputed by these men as sin, but it is not even a sin among them.[32]

To all this Bellarmine answers forcefully: "Civil law obliges in conscience no less than divine law does." [33] For, he explains, the force of obligation is of the very essence of law. To oblige is a necessary effect of law. Therefore any law, whether from God or an angel or man, and whether the man is a bishop or a king or a father, obliges in exactly the same way.[34]

Why does obligation follow from the very essence of law? Because, Bellarmine insists, "law is a rule of action, and it is proper to a rule to direct intrinsically. As a consequence, any deviation from the rule is a sin; just as a deviation from the rule in natural things is called a sin of nature (for instance, a monster), and a deviation from the rule of art is called a sin of art." [35]

Now what Bellarmine has said is, if laws oblige because they direct intrinsically to an end, that the foundation of obligation is the necessary relation of means to an end. For, to deviate from the law is not to attain the end, and that is a sin. Bellarmine knew St. Thomas too well not to

[32] *De sacramento baptismi*, I, c. 16, 269B.

[33] *De laicis*, III, c. 11, 471C.

[34] *Ibid.*, 471D. Cf. *De romano pont.*, IV, c. 16, 856D-E.

[35] *Loc. cit.* It is interesting, at this point, to compare Bellarmine's idea of justice and rectitude with that of Anselm. Bellarmine says that ". . . justice, whence justification has its name, is nothing else than the rectitude of *order*. For that is just which is right and adequate and most conformable with its *rule"* (*De justificatione*, I, c. 1, 700E). Anselm says: "That will, therefore, must be called just which preserves its rectitude on account of rectitude itself. . . . Justice, therefore, is the rectitude of the will preserved *on account of itself"* (*De veritate*, c. 12 [*PL*, CLVIII, 482]) (italics added). Cf. above, chap. 1.

recognize the relation between Ia, q. 82, a. 1 and Ia IIae, q. 21, a. 1 of the *Summa theologiae*. For Bellarmine, as for St. Thomas, it is in terms of the end and the relation of means thereunto, that law, obligation, and sin have their ultimate meaning.

What will lead to an end (in other words, what will perfect a being) is already determined by the very form and nature of the being. For, as Bellarmine says, "just as other things depend upon an agent for their existence but not for their essence (for essences are eternal since they are possible participations of the divine essence), so law as to its existence depends upon a legislator . . . but as to its essence it does not. That law should oblige is something eternal and immutable, for it is a participation in the eternal law of God, which is the first and highest rule." [36]

Thus, though the existence of a law may depend on the decision of a lawgiver, the fact that it will oblige does not. This is determined by the relation of the essence of the means commanded by the law to the end. And although, Bellarmine says stressing the point, it really could not happen that a true law would not be from God, since law cannot be established except by one having authority and authority is only from God, nevertheless "if (*per impossibile*) there were a law that was not from God, even so it would oblige, because this is the intrinsic nature of law. Just as if (*per impossibile*) a man should exist not made by God, even so he would be rational, because that is the very nature of man." [37]

[36] *Ibid.,* 471 E.
[37] *Loc. cit.*

Therefore Bellarmine says once and for all: "Although it may depend upon the legislator whether he will truly command and establish a law or only indicate what should be done, nevertheless, if he seriously wishes to command, it is not in his power to decide whether the law obliges or not." It necessarily obliges, under pain of mortal or venial sin according to the nature of the acts involved.[38]

Therefore, not only is the objective nature of the acts commanded by law the foundation of obligation, but it is also the fact which determines how serious the obligation will be. Human law, just as divine law, obliges under pain of mortal or venial sin, depending upon the gravity of the acts themselves.[39]

If, Bellarmine adds, a law obliged solely because it was divine and not on account of the very nature of the acts themselves, all divine laws would oblige equally. The same reason for obligation would be found in all of them. But this is false because the law, "Thou shalt not kill," obliges more than the law, "Thou shalt not steal"; and the law, "Thou shalt not steal," obliges more than the law, "Thou shalt not lie"; and the law, "Thou shalt not lie," obliges more than the law, "Thou shalt not speak an idle word."[40] Thus the importance of the objective essences of acts receives full recognition in Bellarmine.

Why does the nature of the acts commanded by law both induce obligation and determine the degree of obligation? Because, Bellarmine says, an act by its very nature either leads to the end or away from it, wholly or par-

[38] *Ibid.*, 474C.
[39] *Ibid.*, 471C. Cf. *De amiss. grat. et stat. pecc.*, III, c. 10, 183B.
[40] *De laicis*, III, c. 11, 472A.

tially.[41] Therefore obligation under pain of mortal or venial sin is defined in terms of the nature of acts and their relation to the end.

Because of Bellarmine's stress on the importance of finality in law, he has no difficulty in establishing a perfect integration of all species of law. For all law, as he has said, is but a participation in the directing of the eternal law. Therefore, since ultimately they all have the same end, they all oblige in conscience. Any transgression of the natural, or of the positive, or of the divine, or of the human law is a sin against the eternal law.[42] In other words, the idea of law being analogous is perfectly established in Bellarmine.

For Bellarmine, then, the civil law cannot be without moral content. Civil law is only a conclusion or determination of the divine moral law. Both have the same end ultimately. They differ only in this: Human law directs and orders human acts to acts of external love, that is, to the peace and preservation of the community. Divine law directs acts to acts of internal love, that is, to charity. Therefore both divine law and human law oblige for the same reason, the relation of what they command to an end.[43]

Hence Bellarmine's thought has no place for a separation of the civil from the moral order. A *peccatum philosophicum* would be for him the sheerest nonsense, such as might be expected perhaps from a Calvin or a Luther.

But now an important difficulty presents itself. If obli-

[41] *De amiss. grat. et stat. pecc.,* I, c. 14, 95C.
[42] *De laicis,* III, c. 11, 471E.
[43] *Ibid.,* 472B.

gation and its degree of gravity come from the nature of the act and its relation to an end, then laws are superfluous. For, if the act by its very nature is necessary for the end, then there is an obligation to perform it even before the law commands it. Hence a law commanding the act is superfluous.[44]

Bellarmine's answer clarifies the distinction between what is good or bad for this or that man, and what is good or bad for the whole community. For, Bellarmine says, if there is no law commanding something in general, there will be many things which will be evil to one and not evil to another. For instance, if there were no law forbidding the carrying of arms, the carrying of arms would be evil for him who is easily provoked to anger and who has enemies he wishes to kill. On the other hand, the carrying of arms would not be an evil to the peaceful man who desires only to defend himself. Nevertheless, if the law forbids it, the carrying of arms is an evil for all. For law should not consider what is good or evil for this or that man. Rather it should be concerned with what helps or hinders the community.[45]

Besides, Bellarmine continues, there are many things which are necessary or harmful to the common good which nevertheless are not good or evil to this or that one in particular, unless it be commanded by law. For instance, it is necessary to pay taxes to the king. Yet, if there were no such law, it would not be necessary that I pay the taxes. For, my individual contribution would mean little

[44] *Ibid.*, 472C.
[45] *Loc. cit.*

to the king. Nor does it pertain to me to see which things the community needs; and all others could say the same. Similarly, it is harmful to the community to export gold out of the country. But it is not notably harmful that I alone export my gold; and again all others could say the same thing. Therefore law is necessary which, commanding and forbidding in general, considers the public utility.[46]

But does Bellarmine mean that such acts are indifferent in themselves and become good or bad, and therefore obligatory, simply because they are commanded by law?

Let us see. Bellarmine says that the divine positive law obliges under pain of sin because it constitutes an act as good which previously was not. If a Jew, for example, had moderately eaten pork (an act forbidden by law), not from contempt but because of his appetite for food, without doubt he would have sinned. But he would not have sinned formally against obedience, because he did not act out of contempt. Therefore it must have been because it was against temperance. But again, to eat pork moderately is not of itself against temperance, because it is an indifferent act. Therefore it was the law that made this abstinence a necessary act of temperance.[47]

This, says Bellarmine, is exactly the case in human law. The divine law makes good an act that in itself was indifferent, for no other reason than because the divine law is a rule of moral action established by Him who has the authority to command. But man can also command and estab-

46 *Ibid.*, 472D.
47 *Ibid.*, 472E.

lish rules of moral action. Therefore man by his law can constitute an act as good which before was indifferent. Thus both divine law and human law are equally obligatory.[48]

Again Bellarmine says that whoever can command, can by his command make necessary and *per se* good an act that was indifferent. But to omit an act that is necessary and *per se* good is a sin in conscience, even without contempt or scandal.[49] For an indifferent act, if it is commanded, becomes necessary. Otherwise the command is in vain. This is proved *a posteriori;* since otherwise it would follow that the positive laws of God would not oblige in conscience. Why does circumcision oblige the Jews and why does baptism oblige us, since these are in themselves indifferent acts? God, however, does not thus oblige inasmuch as He is God, but only inasmuch as He is a legislator. And whoever can command, especially in the name of God, can do the same thing.[50]

A true law, then, can make necessary an act of virtue which was not necessary before, since it determines and commands that it be done.[51]

Finally, in contrasting the law of peoples with civil law, Bellarmine says that what is prohibited by the law of peoples is prohibited because it is evil; whereas what is forbidden by the civil law, since it is purely positive, is evil because prohibited.[52]

48 *Loc. cit.*
49 *De romano pont.,* IV, c.16, 847D.
50 *Ibid.,* 847E.
51 *De bonis operibus in partic.,* II, c.7, 1086A.
52 *De clericis,* I, c.29, 297C. The use of the phrase "law of peoples" is intended here as a noncommittal translation of the controversial expression *jus*

This series of statements seems to be in direct contradiction to the principles which Bellarmine has already laid down, namely, that the necessity and obligation of placing an act is determined by the nature of the act itself and its consequent relation to an end. There would be cause for some concern in regard to the way Bellarmine has been expressing himself if it were not for two facts: first, he holds that there are no indifferent acts *in concreto;* and secondly, he has already explained what he means by "indifferent" acts in the community.

Thus Bellarmine, with St. Thomas, maintains that *in concreto* there can be no such thing as an indifferent act. As soon as an act comes under consideration for action, it is always in relation to a certain end. This end must be good or bad; there are no indifferent ends. Hence *in concreto* no act can be indifferent. It is either good or bad. Therefore acts are necessarily specified as good or bad from the end and the intention thereunto.[53]

And, as he has already explained, certain acts (for instance, carrying arms) are good or bad for this or that individual person taken singly. As such, because of their relative unimportance in these isolated instances, they may be considered "indifferent" to the common good. When, however, these acts are considered as possible actions for all the members of the community, they lose their so-called "indifference" and become in general good or bad acts, contributing to the common good or detract-

gentium. For a history of the development of the concept of the *jus gentium,* cf. C. a Vlissingen, *De evolutione definitionis iuris gentium* (Rome: Gregorian University, 1940).

[53] *De effectu sacrament.,* II, c.32, 205D.

ing from it. Further, it should be noted that all the examples given by Bellarmine of these "indifferent" acts are not without some definite meaning and value in themselves: carrying arms, exporting gold, contributing to the support of the government, abstaining from pork, circumcision, or baptism (a cleansing).[54]

It is with these facts in mind, then, that we must understand Bellarmine's statement, that the command of law makes an indifferent act good or bad.

With these principles of law and obligation well established, to respond to the difficulties of his adversaries was not hard for Bellarmine.

For one with civil authority to oblige a subject in conscience, it is not necessary that he be able to penetrate the subject's conscience. It suffices that he be able to command the subject legitimately, and by commanding so to oblige him to the performance of external acts that if he does not do them he knows or can know that he does wrong.[55] It is true, Bellarmine says, that political power is temporal, that its end is exterior peace, and that man cannot judge about internal things. But this does not mean that civil authority cannot oblige in conscience. For, although the

---

[54] Thus, in regard to eating pork, the commentary on Lev. 11:2 (Douay Version) says: ". . . the things here forbidden were for the most part unwholesome and not proper to be eaten."

In regard to circumcision, utilitarian motives, such as cleanliness, freedom from disease, offspring, have always accompanied religious ones. "Like the law of clean and unclean, in food and daily life, it [circumcision] may be regarded as a practice of venerable antiquity that was adopted and adapted to express what it had not expressed before, . . . the same as is true of lustral water" (J. T. Tierney, "Circumcision," *The Catholic Encyclopedia*, III, 777).

[55] *De romano pont.*, IV, c.20, 864C-D.

rule directs exterior acts, nevertheless, because it is a rule, to deviate from it is a sin.[56]

How can temporal authority produce a spiritual effect, that is, oblige in conscience? Bellarmine answers that, although political power and its law are called temporal by reason of their object, which is concerned with temporal or exterior things, nevertheless "in themselves they are spiritual things." Besides, he adds, to oblige in conscience is not to effect something on a spiritual thing. "It is only to command another, and so to command that if he does not obey, he sins. By the testimony of his own conscience he knows or can know that he sins." [57] Therefore, to deviate from any law, because it is a rule constituted by God either immediately or mediately, is a sin.[58]

Purely penal law? Such a position could not help bringing forth violent objections from those who wished to hold purely penal law, not only from the followers of Calvin and Luther, but also from many of his own religious confreres.[59]

But Bellarmine had already resolutely taken his stand on the nature of law and obligation: that they are essentially concerned with the essences of things and their relation as means necessary to an end. Any deviation from law which commanded such means was *eo ipso* a sin. With such a view of reality, Bellarmine could see no reason why a person should be punished unless it was because he had

[56] *De laicis,* III, c. 11, 473E.
[57] *Loc. cit.*
[58] *De romano pont.,* IV, c. 16, 856D.
[59] Cf., e.g., above, Suarez, chap. 6.

committed a fault. *"Culpa* and *poena* are relative terms."
Otherwise punishment is irrational, a contradiction.
Hence, to speak of a law that does not oblige in conscience
to what is commanded but only to the undergoing of punishment is, for Bellarmine, a contradiction.[60] In fact, the
only objective justification for the severity of just punishment is the gravity of the preceding fault.[61]

But what of the ever-present objection of the proponents of purely penal law, that it is a legitimate notion because the rules of religious unions are such: they oblige
acceptance of the punishment, and do not oblige under
pain of fault or sin? [62] Bellarmine answers as he must answer, in view of the principles he has already set down.
The rules of religious unions "do not oblige after the manner of a law, but only as agreements or pacts." In this sense
only, they may be called purely penal "laws." Nor is the
punishment inflicted by these rules punishment properly
so called, because no fault has been previously committed.
Rather it is a "penal affliction accepted for the good of the
spirit." [63] Hence the rules of religious unions are not,
strictly speaking, laws.

What then of the decisions of the councils, and what
about canon law? Are they true laws? Since, as he says, "it
is difficult to find more than four laws imposed absolutely
on all Christians (observe feasts, keep the fasts, confess
once a year, and receive Communion during the paschal
season)," the rest would not seem to be true laws. The so-

60 *De laicis*, III, c.11, 473C.
61 *De romano pont.*, IV, c.16, 847B. Cf. *ibid.*, 848E.
62 *De laicis*, III, c.11, 473C.
63 *Loc. cit.*

called "laws" in the "tomes of the councils and the books of canon law are not laws, but are either admonitions or pious instructions which do not oblige in conscience under pain of sin. Such are a large number of Christian rites." [64]

These statements of Bellarmine in regard to the status of "law" in religious unions and canon law show unmistakably how foreign to his thought was the concept of purely penal law.

Bellarmine, then, was a man who understood St. Thomas well. Hence he clearly saw that the intellect was man's superior power. If man's form was intellectual, then the will must desire the good of man as such. Therefore it must ultimately desire man's intellectual good.

Bellarmine firmly grasped the causal relation of the intellect and the will in the act of decision, the judgment of election. For him, then, there was no false problem in regard to the intellect physically necessitating the will. Hence neither was there a problem for Bellarmine in regard to the intellect morally necessitating the will. The command, which was the essence of law, was of the intellect. Therefore law was an act of the intellect. Hence law obliged because what it commanded was a means objectively necessary for the common good. Obligation, moral necessity, was founded upon this objective necessity of means to end.

[64] *De romano pont.*, IV, c.18, 861D-E. If Bellarmine is right, then certain canons which are now included in the body of canon law as true laws are not laws at all. Cf. Vermeersch-Creusen, *Epitome iuris canonici* (Rome, 1933), pp. 96 ff.; Wernz-Vidal, *Ius canonicum* (Rome, 1938), pp. 212 ff.

This being the case, whatever law commanded obliged in conscience. Hence the concept of purely penal law, which obliged only to the payment of the penalty, was inadmissible. Certain things called laws (such as the rules of religious unions, or many things in the councils and in canon law) are not true laws. They are agreements, admonitions, or instructions.

The opinion may be ventured that Bellarmine, because he explains the act of election so well, knew the thought of St. Thomas better than the other commentators whom we have been here considering. Cajetan and Medina, as Soto rightly charged, put the command before the election, thereby destroying liberty. Soto himself, trying to preserve liberty, put the last act of the intellect before the election in the judgment of *synesis*. But in doing so he failed to maintain intellectual causality in the act of election. The election became a purely volitional act. Bellarmine, however, saw that the act of election was an act of the appetitive intellect or of the intellective appetite; it was a judged election or an elected judgment.[65] Consequently the command was, for Bellarmine, an act that followed the election and directed the executive powers in their carrying out of the means already elected.

Bellarmine's philosophy of intellect and will was without internal difficulties, and therefore left the way open for a concept of law that was intellectual and a concept of obligation that was based upon the objective essences of things and their relation to the end.

[65] Cf. above, chap. 8.

CONSEQUENCES

SUCH, then, are the two concepts of law and obligation which have developed during the past six hundred years. In the one, law is an act of the intellect because law is concerned with the relation and order of means necessary for an end, and only the intellect can perceive such a relation. Obligation, consequently, is founded upon this relation. In the other concept, law is an act of the will because the establishment of such a relation of order must be the work of the will, there being no act of the intellect after the election to which this ordering could be attributed. Hence obligation can have no source but the will itself.

The growth of these two concepts has been gradual. The one favoring the primacy of the will, with roots in Augustine and Anselm, was given incipient form by Henry of Ghent. Henry made the will superior because, he said, its object and its acts were prime. The will may follow the intellect if it so chooses, as the master may follow the servant lighting the way if he so desires. In fact, the will may direct the intellect. This being the case, the act of command and law itself pertain to the will. Whether a law will oblige or not depends upon the will of the lawgiver. Obligation therefore has it source in the will, and purely penal law is a logical consequence.

Scotus, with a more penetrating insight perhaps than

most of the men we have treated, attacked the problem of the nature of the intellect and will at its vital point: finality. The uniqueness of the will, he said, in contradistinction to nature, consisted in its freedom. It is free even in regard to its end. Man, for Scotus, was essentially a free being. No physical or moral necessity could be placed upon the will. The will is not only supreme, it is autonomous. Hence the acts of ordering (*ordinare*) and commanding must come from the will alone. Law, therefore, pertains to the will, and therein is found the source of obligation. The consequence of this fact is that acts, of their very nature, do not necessarily have a relation to the end. The precepts of the second table of the Decalogue, for instance, oblige only because God so wills.

For Ockham, in accord with his theory of signification, the act of the soul willing was superior to the act of the soul knowing. For the act of love is nobler than the act of knowing. Hence no necessity, physical or moral, can be imposed upon the soul willing. The act of command, then, must pertain to the will. Consequently law pertains to the will, and its power of obliging derives solely from the will of the lawgiver. The ultimate and very logical conclusion, according to these principles, is reached when Ockham says that even if God should will that the hatred of Himself be a good act, then it would be a good act.

Biel, following Ockham, also holds that the act of the soul willing is nobler than the act of the soul knowing. The principal reason why this is true is that freedom is in the will. With the act of command inevitably pertaining to the will, law is a sign of reason willing to oblige. Consequently murder and adultery, for instance, are bad only because forbidden by command of the divine will. With obligation thus depending on the will of the lawgiver, he could choose to pass a law which did not oblige in conscience, a purely penal law.

Castro brought the philosophy of the primacy of the will to bear directly on the theory of purely penal law. If the acts of ordering (*ordinare*) and command pertain to the will, Castro logically concluded that so also did law and obligation. As a result, law is defined as the right will of the lawgiver, obligation derives from this will, and purely penal law is the practical consequence.

Suarez calls upon all these men for support of his position. The will is the superior power. After the election, no other act is necessary. Hence command is the same as, or is included in, the election. This means that the will can order and direct. Hence law is an act of a just and right will, and obligation takes its force therefrom. Hence purely penal law is true law. Suarez attempts to work into his concept of obligation the necessity of a common good, with the result that he ultimately becomes involved in a contradiction.

The other concept, giving superiority to the intellect, entails a totally different view of man. For Albert the Great, man is essentially a knowing being. Without information by the intellect, the will is not the will but only a confused appetite. This fact necessitates a mutual causal interrelation between the intellect and will. The act following the election (the impetus or command) pertains to the intellect, because it directs the means elected to the end. Hence law is an act of the intellect, and obligation must be based on the objective nature of the acts which are the objects of the intellect.

St. Thomas holds the intellect to be superior to the will because its object is more simple and absolute. The will's act of election is possible only because of the fact that the intellect is capable of diverse conceptions of the good. Hence, whereas the act of election pertains essentially to the will, when considered in relation to its dependence on the intellect, the will's causality in the election is material and the intellect's is formal. After the election of the means, an act directing the execution of these means to the end is necessary. This is the command, which pertains essentially to the intellect. In relation, however, to the previous act of the will, the intellect's causality in the act of the command is material; that of the will is formal. Because command belongs to the intellect, so does law. And because it is the objective nature of things that specifies the intellect and the intellect exercises mutual causality with the will, the source of moral necessity or obligation in the will is the objective nature of acts and their rela-tion to the end. According to these principles, all laws oblige in conscience to the acts commanded, and conse-quently the concept of purely penal civil law is not in St. Thomas.

Cajetan in general follows St. Thomas in his psychology and philosophy of law. The intellect is the nobler faculty. The act of *ordinare*, and therefore the command, pertains to the intellect. Law is an act of the intellect, and obliga-tion is based upon the order of means to the end. Cajetan has difficulty in explaining the act of command, but this does not undermine his intellectual foundation for his concept of law. There is no evidence that Cajetan held the concept of purely penal civil law.

Soto also follows St. Thomas closely in his concept of the intellect and will and of law. The intellect is the predominant faculty, and command is an act of the intellect. Consequently law is an act of the intellect. Obligation is founded upon the objective nature of acts, and a law obliges even if the lawgiver does not mention whether the law obliges or not. Hence Soto, refusing to believe that there can be a *poena* without a *culpa*, rejects the concept of purely penal civil law. The so-called "laws" of religious orders are, he says, rather agreements or pacts upon which one voluntarily enters.

Medina is extremely insistent upon the primacy of the intellect. When the intellect commands the will to elect, there is no alternative for the will but to act. Law, then, could be an act only of the intellect. The source of obligation is so far removed from the intention of the lawgiver and so completely founded on the objective nature of acts, that even if the lawgiver does not think of obliging his subjects, the law nevertheless obliges. Medina therefore emphatically rejects the theory of purely penal civil law and adds that, in his opinion, the so-called "laws" of religious orders are not laws in the true sense of the word.

Bellarmine, who seems to have known the mind of St. Thomas better than any of the men we have been considering, holds that the intellect is the higher power, because the will is a *rational* appetite and therefore the cause of liberty is in the intellect itself. The act of election is, then, an act in which both the intellect and the will participate. Bellarmine has grasped the full meaning of St. Thomas' *judicium electionis*. And since the act of directing pertains to the intellect and since there is need of an act after the election to direct the execution of the means elected to the end, there is need of the intellectual act of command. Law then pertains to the intellect, and obligation has its source in the necessary relation of means to the end. The legislator may decide whether a law should be established or not, but it is not in his power to decide whether or not it will oblige. Consequently, since every *poena* must suppose a *culpa,* the theory of purely penal civil law is self-contradictory. The "laws" of religious unions are in truth only pacts, and many things now accepted as laws (for instance, in canon law) are not true laws, but only admonitions or instructions.

It is thus in the diverse philosophies of intellect and will that the ultimate solution of the problem of law and obligation must be sought. This entails the most basic interpretation of man. Is man essentially a free being, or is he essentially a knowing being? Which is the superior faculty, the will or the intellect? Is the will completely independent of any necessity imposed by the intellect, or is it metaphysically dependent upon such an interaction of the intellect? Is the part played by the intellect in the election only that of a *conditio sine qua non* for the action of the will, or is it that of a true mutual cause? Is the perception of the relation and order between means to an end a function of the will, or is it solely the prerogative of the intellect? In a word, is the will solely an active potency in no way subject to any influence outside of itself; or it is not only an active potency (for it is the sole efficient cause of the human act) but also a passive potency penetrated by the influence of the rational? [1]

These are some of the questions that lie at the bottom of the profound divergences of the two philosophies of intellect and will, and therefore of the two concepts of law and obligation.

The results of these differences on the practical level issue in what are, for all intents and purposes, two totally different views of civil life. In the one view, because obligation comes from the will of the lawgiver, there may be purely penal civil laws which do not oblige in conscience to what the law commands but only to the payment of the penalty in case of violation. If this is true, then there is a vast segment of civil life that a man is not obliged to consider seriously as pertaining to his conscience. Such violations may be "wrong," but they are not bad or sin.

In the other view, since obligation derives from the relation of means (taken in their objective nature) to the end, no such thing as a purely penal civil law is possible. All laws, if they are true laws, oblige in conscience: if not under pain of mortal at least under that of venial sin. Hence a citizen's whole civic life is a matter concerning conscience, either gravely or, as is perhaps mostly the case, only slightly.[2] A violation of law is wrong and is therefore

[1] Cf. O. Lottin, *Psychologie et morale aux XII e et XIII e siècles,* Tome III, Part 2 (Louvain: Mt. César, 1949), pp. 651–66.

[2] An interesting point of speculation is whether, if the latter doctrine had been consistently taught for the last six hundred years and men had been

a bad act and consequently some kind of sin, grave or slight.[3]

If the relation between the concept of law and the philosophy of intellect and will is direct and immediate, as we have seen it to be, then there is a glaring inconsistency facing us today. Many who hold Aquinas' and Bellarmine's philosophy of intellect and will are holding Scotus' and Suarez' concept of law and obligation. A glance at most manuals of moral theology and canon law will offer sufficient confirmation. This means only that many are not yet aware of the contradiction here involved nor are they fully cognizant of the relation between psychology and law. Those who feel that there is something wrong with purely penal law are inclined to locate it in the difficulty of knowing the intention of the lawgiver,[4] instead of calling into question the validity of the very notion of purely penal civil law.[5] To do this, however, requires a recognition of the fact that the problem has profound psychological implications. This can be obtained only from acquaintance with the history of the development of the

---

shown their full obligation in civil life, it would have been as necessary for recent pontiffs to insist repeatedly that certain aspects of civil life oblige in conscience.

[3] If this is thought to be burdensome, it must be remembered that laws should be concerned only with what is somehow necessary for the common good and that *epikeia* has a legitimate place in the interpretation of laws. Besides, those who hold purely penal law say that each violation ordinarily involves a sin of contempt of authority or of disobedience. Cf. above, Suarez, chap. 6.

[4] Cf., for instance, *Theological Studies*, March 1947, p. 111. On the invalidity of the supposition that lawgivers actually intend or do not intend to oblige when they make laws, see L. Ulpianas, S.J., "Theoria legis mere poenalis et hodiernae leges civiles," *Periodica*, XXVII (1938), 203.

[5] See the very informative article by A. Van Hove, "Quelques publications récentes au sujet des lois purement pénales," *Miscellanea Moralia* (Louvain, 1948) pp. 225-53.

concept of law as related to a philosophy of intellect and will.

To be sure, the problem is truly complicated. Related to it are other, shall we say, subsidiary problems. For instance: Why are some men attracted ultimately to the primacy of the will, others to the primacy of the intellect? Is it because of doctrinal or historical reasons? What was the full reason why, after the condemnation of 1270, St. Thomas rewrote, to some extent at least, that part of his psychology which pertains to the election?[6] How much was Scotus influenced in regard to the primacy of the will by this condemnation? Why did Suarez change his position from a command of the intellect in his earlier writings to a command of the will in his later works?[7] Was this related to the controversy *De auxiliis* then raging? How much was he influenced by contemporary misrepresentations of Thomism?

Then there are other problems: What is the history of the distinction between the "necessary" and the "useful" and their relation to the common good? Why has the distinction between what is "relatively necessary" (as opposed to "absolutely necessary") and the merely "useful" not been more completely recognized and worked out? Does the distinction between "necessity of means" and "necessity of precept" presuppose one of the philosophical positions that we have been considering? What are the full consequences of these two philosophies of intellect and will in regard to prayer, vow, and contract—which

---

6 Cf. above, chap. 8.
7 Cf. above, chap. 6, note 19.

St. Thomas and also Suarez say are fundamentally the same problem as law? Lastly, what is the impact of these different philosophies on the problem of love? [8]

Evidently the labor of many heads and hands will be required before these and many other problems can be solved and their relation to psychology and law more fully determined. It is here, so it seems, that much of the effort of our research should be centered. If the multiplicity involved in these various questions is ever to be reduced to unity, it must be done by some unifying principle. And this unifying principle can be only the true nature of man, of his intellect and will. [9]

The concept of law is one of the noblest ever to enter the life of man. Its end is to remake man, to make him good. It is law which means the difference between disorder and order, between wrong and right, between bad and good, between injustice and justice, between war and peace. Yes, it is that without which man can never hope to understand even himself. For it is only through the concept of law that he is able to grasp fully his participation

[8] Certainly the problem of love cannot be solved by an attempt to compose these two irreconcilable and irreducible positions. Cf., for instance, M. D'Arcy, *Mind and Heart of Love* (New York: Holt, 1948), p. 290.

[9] The contemporary importance of a proper understanding of the nature of the intellect and will and their interrelation has recently been emphasized by the present pontiff in his encyclical *Humani Generis* when, criticizing certain novel opinions, he said: ". . . it is one thing to admit the power of the dispositions of the will in helping reason to gain a more certain and firm knowledge of moral truths; it is quite another thing to say, as these innovators do, indiscriminately mingling cognition and act of will, that the appetitive and affective faculties have a *certain power of understanding*, and that man, since he cannot by using his reason decide with certainty what is true and is to be accepted, turns to his will, by which he freely chooses among opposite opinions" (italics added).

in the divine ordering and governance of all things, the eternal law.

St. Thomas' philosophy of law and obligation has never had the proponent and advocate that Scotus' philosophy has had in a man like Suarez. No one has yet written a truly Thomistically inspired *De legibus* of the scope and influence of Suarez' work. The complete presentation of St. Thomas' concept of law and obligation as founded upon his philosophy of intellect and will is the great work yet to be done.

Hence, what Professor Gilson has said in regard to St. Thomas' philosophy of existence seems quite true also of St. Thomas' philosophy of law. Whatever be the reasons, Professor Gilson says, "it is a fact that the example given by St. Thomas Aquinas has found but few imitators. Many have commented on him, but few have followed him. The only manner of truly following him would be to redo his work such as he himself would do today, starting from the same principles and going further than he did, in the same direction and on the same road that he has already opened. If these principles are true, then certainly their fecundity has not been exhausted. There is therefore nothing absurd in putting them to work again in the hope that they will throw some light on the aspects of the real that they were, in their first formulation, destined to clarify." [10]

10 Étienne Gilson, *L'Être et l'essence* (Paris: Vrin, 1948), p. 321.

BIBLIOGRAPHY

Primary Sources

Albert the Great, O.P., St. *Opera omnia,* ed. by P. Jammy
(Lyons, 1651); ed. by A. Borgnet (Paris: Vivés, 1890–
99).

Anselm of Canterbury, St. *Opera omnia nec non eadmeri
monachi historia novorum et alia opuscula,* labore ac
studio D. G. Gerberon (Paris: Migne, 1863).

————. *Fides quaerens intellectum id est Proslogion, Liber Guanilonis pro insipiente atque Liber apologeti-
cus contra Guanilonem,* texte et traduction par A.
Koyre (Paris: Vrin, 1930).

————. *Proslogium; Monologium; An Appendix in Be-
half of the Fool by Guanilon; and Cur Deus Homo,*
trans. by Sidney Norton Deane (Chicago: Open
Court Publishing Co., 1930).

Aristotle. *Opera omnia,* ed. by Firmin-Didot (Paris,
1883).

————. *Opera omnia,* ed. by Maurus-Ehrle (Paris: Lethielleux, 1885).

————. *De justitia Aristotelis ethicorum ad Nichoma-
chum,* ed. by Maurus-Schuster (Rome, 1934).

Augustine, St. *Opera omnia* (Lyons, 1664).

————. *Opera omnia* . . . opera et studio Monachorum
Ord. S. Benedicti, editio emendata accurate J. P.
Migne (Paris, 1841).

————. *Opera omnia*, in *Patrologiae cursus completus, Series Latina*, XXXII–XL, ed. by J. P. Migne (Paris, 1877–90).

————. *De eudaimonia sive de beatitudine*, textus ex philosophis antiquis collegit atque introductionibus et notis illustravit J. B. Schuster, S.J. (Rome: Gregorian University, 1933).

————. *Contra academicos libri tres*, in *Corpus Scriptorum Eccles. Latinorum*, LXIII, ed. by Tempsky (Vienna, 1922).

Averroes. *Opera omnia Aristotelis Stagiritae cum Averrois Cordubensis commentariis* (Venice: Junta, 1574).

Azpilcueta, Martin (Navarrus). *Consiliorum sive responsorum* (Cremona, 1591).

————. *Enchiridion, sive manuale confessariorum et poenitentium* (Rome, 1588; Wirceburg, 1593; Antwerp, 1617).

————. *Commentarius de usuris* (Rome, 1588).

Bañez, Domingo, O.P. *Commentarios ineditos a la Prima Secundae de Santo Tomás* (Madrid, 1942).

————. *Scholastica commentaria in Iam partem D. Thomae* (Douay, 1614).

Bellarmine, St. Robert, S.J. *Disputationes . . . de controversiis Christianae fidei adversus huius temporis haereticos* (Venice, 1599).

————. *Opera omnia* (Naples, 1872).

————. *Opera omnia*, ed. by Vivés (Paris, 1883).

————. *Opera oratoria postuma*, ed. by Tromp (Rome: Gregorian University, 1942).

————. *Breve dottrina Cristiana* (Naples, 1837).

————. *De cognitione Dei* (Louvain: Fonteyn, 1861).

Biel, Gabriel. *Epythoma pariter et collectorium circa quatuor Sententiarum libros* (Tübingen, 1501).

————. *Supplementum in XXVII distinctiones ultimas Sententiarum* (Tübingen, 1520).

————. *Treatise on the Power and Utility of Moneys,* translated by R. B. Burke (London: Oxford University Press, 1930).

Bonaventure, St., O.F.M. *Opera omnia,* edita studio et cura PP. Collegii a S. Bonaventura (Quaracchi: Typographia Collegii S. Bonaventurae, 1882–1902).

————. *Commentaria in quatuor libros Sententiarum Magistri Petri Lombardi* (Quaracchi, 1882).

————. *Breviloquium adjectis illustrationibus ex aliis operibus eiusdem S. Doct. Depromptis,* P. Antonius Maria a Vicetia, ed. (editio altera, Freiburg i. Br.: Herder, 1881).

————. *Breviloquium et itinerarium mentis ad Deum* (Tübingen, 1861).

Cajetan (Thomas de Vio), O.P. *Commentaria in Summam Theologicam S. Thomae* (Antwerp, 1568; Leonine ed., Rome, 1888–1906).

————. *Opuscula* (Venice, 1588).

————. *S. Thomae Summa theologica cum commentariis Thomae Card. Cajetani* et elucidationibus litteralibus P. Seraphini Capponi a Porrecta (Rome, 1773).

————. *Tractatus de subjecto naturalis philosophiae,* ed. by C. de Koninck (Quebec: Laval University, 1939).

————. *De nominum analogia* (Quebec: Laval University, 1942).

Capreolus, John, O.P. *Defensiones theologiae divi Thomae,* de novo editae cura et studio C. Paban et T. Pegues (Turin, 1900).

Castro, Alfonso de, O.F.M. *La Fuerza de la Ley Penal,* trans. by Gallego (Univ. de Murcia, 1931).

————. *Opera* (Paris, 1571).

Damascene, St. John. *Opera omnia,* in *Patrologiae cursus completus, Series Graeca,* XCIV–XCVI, ed. by J. P. Migne.

Gerson, John. *Opera omnia,* ed. by Ellies du Pin (Antwerp, 1706).

Grotius, Hugo. *De jure belli ac pacis,* G. Fritsch (Amsterdam, 1735).

Henry of Ghent. *Aurea quodlibeta,* hac postrema editione commentariis doctissimis illustrata M. Vitalis Zuccolii Patavini. Apud Jacobum de Franciscis (Paris, 1518; Venice, 1613).

————. *Summa in tres partes praecipuas digesta . . .* opera et studio A. R. P. M. Hieronymi Scarparii. Apud Franciscum succium (Ferrara, 1646).

————. *Summae quaestionum ordinariarum . . .* (Paris: Ascensius, 1520).

Kant, Immanuel. *Immanuel Kant's Werke,* ed. by Cassirer (Berlin, 1922).

Medina, Bartholomew, O.P. *Expositio in Primam Secundae Angelici Doctoris D. Thomae Aquinatis* (Salamanca, 1582).

Ockham, William, O.F.M. *Super quatuor libros senten-tiarum subtilissimae quaestiones earumque deci-siones* (Lyons, 1495).

———. *Quodlibeta septem una cum tractatu de sacra-mento altaris* . . . (Strassburg, 1491).

———. *De Sacramento altaris et de corpore Christi,* trans. by T. B. Birch (Burlington, Iowa: The Lutheran Literary Board, 1930).

———. *Breviloquium de potestate papae,* ed. by L. Bau-dry (Paris: Vrin, 1937).

———. *La tractatus de principiis theologiae,* attribué à G. d'Occam, ed. by L. Baudry (Paris: Vrin, 1936).

Scotus, John Duns, O.F.M. *Opera omnia,* edited by Wad-ding (Lyons, 1639); reprinted by Vivés (Paris, 1891–95).

———. *Commentaria Oxoniensia ad IV libros* . . . *Sen-tentiarum,* ed. by Garcia (Quaracchi, 1912–14).

———. *Quaestiones disputatae de rerum principio et tractatus de primo rerum omnium principio,* ed. by Garcia (Quaracchi, 1910).

———. *Les commentaires de Jean Duns Scot sur les quatre livres des sentences,* étude historique et cri-tique (Louvain: Bureaux de la revue, 1927).

Soto, Dominic, O.P. *De justitia et jure.* Apud haeredes Ioannis Antonii Bertani (Venice, 1602).

Suarez, Francis, S.J. *Tractatus de legibus ac Deo legis-latore* (Venice: Coletus, 1740).

———. *Tractatus quinque ad Primam Secundae D. Tho-mae,* ed. by Alvarez (Venice: Coletus, 1740).

―――. *Commentarium in Primam Partem D. Thomae* (Lyons, 1610).

―――. *Metaphysicarum disputationum tomi duo* (Venice: Sessa, 1610).

―――. *De religione* (Lyons: Cardon-Cavellat, 1624).

―――. *De angelis* (Lyons: Cardon-Cavellat, 1610).

―――. *De Deo effectore creaturarum omnium* (Venice: Coletus, 1740).

―――. *De virtute et statu religionis* (Lyons: Cardon, 1609–10).

―――. *De censuris in communi* (Lyons: Cardon, 1618).

―――. *Opus de religione et statu religionis* (Mayence: Mylius, 1609).

―――. *Tractatus theologicus* (Venice: Coletus, 1741).

―――. *Opera omnia* (Paris: Vivés, 1856–78).

―――. *Varia opuscula theologica* (Lyons, 1611).

Sylvester Prierias, O.P. (Mozolini or Mazzolini). *Summa Sylvestrina* (Rome, 1516; Lyons, 1594).

Thomas Aquinas, O.P., St. *Summa theologiae* (Ottawa, 1941).

―――. *Summa contra Gentiles.* Apud Sedem Commissionis Leoninae (Rome, 1934).

―――. *In decem libros Ethicorum Aristotelis ad Nicomachum expositio,* editio novissima cura ac studio p. fr. Angeli M. Pirotta, O.P. (Turin: Domus Editorialis Marietti, 1934).

―――. *In octo libros Politicorum Aristotelis expositio seu De rebus civilibus* (Quebec: Laval, 1940) .

―――. *De Regimine Principum ad Regem Cypri et De*

Regimine Judaeorum ad Ducissam Brabantiae politica opuscula duo (Turin: Domus Editorialis Marietti, 1924).

────. *Opera omnia* (Parma: Fiaccadorus, 1852–73) .

────. *Opera omnia* . . . studio ac labore S. Frette et P. Mare (Paris: Vivés, 1871).

────. *Opera omnia,* iussu impensaque Leonis XIII P. M. (Rome, 1882–1948).

────. *Scriptum super Sententiis Magistri Petri Lombardi* (Paris: Lethielleux, 1933).

────. *Quaestiones disputatae et quaestiones duodecim quodlibetales* (7th ed., Turin: Domus Editorialis Marietti, 1942).

────. *On Kingship,* trans. by Phelan (Toronto: Pontifical Institute, 1949).

Vitoria, Francis, O.P. *Relectiones Morales,* ed. by Simon (Venice, 1696).

────. *Commentarios a la Secunda Secundae de Santo Tomás,* ed. by de Heredia (Salamanca, 1934).

────. *Relectiones Theologicae* (Lyons, 1587).

────. *Relecciones Teologicas* (Madrid, 1934).

Secondary Sources

Books

Association Internationale Vitoria-Suarez. *Vitoria et Suarez: contribution des théologiens au droit international moderne* (Paris: Pedone, 1939).

Baeumker, F. *Die Lehre Anselmes von Kanterbury über den Willen und seine Wahlfreiheit* (Münster i. W.: Aschendorff, 1912).

Baudin, E. *Cours de philosophie morale* (Paris: De Gigord, 1936).

Baudry, Leon. *Le tractatus de principiis theologiae attribué à G. d'Occam* (Paris: Vrin, 1936).

Bender, L., O.P. *Philosophia juris* (Rome: Officium Libri Catholici, 1947).

Boehner, P. *The History of the Franciscan School* (mimeograph, Detroit: Duns Scotus College, 1946).

Bouquillon. *Moral Theology at the End of the 19th Century* (Washington, D.C., 1899).

Bourke, Vernon J. *Augustine's Quest of Wisdom* (Milwaukee: Bruce Publishing Co., 1945).

―――. *St. Thomas and the Greek Moralists* (Milwaukee: Marquette University Press, 1947).

Boyer, Charles, S.J. *Essais sur la doctrine de Saint Augustin* (Paris: Gabriel Beauchesne et ses Fils, 1932).

―――. *Cursus philosophiae* (Paris: Desclée, 1937).

Braun, R. *Die Erkenntnislehre Heinrichs von Gent* (Freiburg [Schweiz], 1916).

Brett, George S. *A History of Psychology* (London: George Allen and Co., 1912).

Breznay, Adalbert. *Clavis theologiae* (Freiburg i. B., 1914).

Brodrick, James, S.J. *The Life and Work of Blessed Robert Francis Cardinal Bellarmine, S.J.* (London: Burns Oates and Washbourne, 1928).

Chevalier, Jacques. *La vie morale et l'au delà* (Paris: Flammarion, 1938).

Dabin, J. *Philosophie de l'ordre juridique positif* (Paris, 1929).

Dahnert, U. *Die Erkenntnislehre des Albertus Magnus* (Leipzig, 1934).

D'Arcy, Martin C. *Mind and Heart of Love* (New York: Holt, 1948).

Delos, J.-T. *La societé internationale et les principes du droit public* (Paris: Pedone, 1929).

Dittrich. *Geschichte der Ethik* (Leipzig: Meiner, 1926).

Felici, P. *De poenali jure interpretando* (Rome: Apollinaris, 1939).

Fessard, Gaston. *Autorité et bien commun* (Paris: Aubier, 1944).

Filliatre, Charles. *La philosophie de Saint Anselme, ses principes, sa nature, son influence* (Paris: Alcan, 1920).

Garcia, Mariano F., O.F.M. *De vita et doctrina B. Joannis Duns Scoti* (7th ed., Quaracchi, 1914).

Garreau, Albert. *Saint Albert le Grand* (Paris: Desclée, 1932).

Getino, Luis G., O.P. *El Maestro Fray Francisco de Vitoria, su vida, su doctrina e influencia* (Madrid, 1903).

Gillet, M. S., O.P. *Notes explicatives, renseignements techniques, sur la Somme Théologique, I–II, qq. 6–21* (Paris: Desclée, 1926).

Gilson, Étienne. *Le Thomisme: Introduction au système de S. Thomas d'Aquin* (Paris: Vrin, 1944).

———. *Saint Thomas d'Aquin* (Paris: Gabalda, 1923).

———. *La philosophie de Saint Bonaventure* (Paris: Vrin, 1924).

———. *Introduction à l'étude de Saint Augustin* (Paris: Vrin, 1931).

——. *Avicenne et le point de départ de Duns Scot* (Paris: Vrin, 1927).

——. *Le moyen âge et le naturalisme antique* (Paris: Vrin, 1933).

——. *Realisme thomiste et critique de la connaissance* (Paris: Vrin, 1939).

——. *The Spirit of Mediaeval Philosophy* (New York: Scribner's, 1936).

——. *La philosophie au moyen âge* (Paris: Payot, 1947).

——. *L'Être et l'essence* (Paris: Vrin, 1948).

Gonet, J. *Clypeus philosophiae thomisticae* (Cologne, 1671).

Gorce, M. M. *L'Essor de la pensée au moyen âge* (Paris: Librairie Letouzey et Ané, 1933).

Grabmann, Martin. *Die Werke des hl. Thomas von Aquin: eine literarhistorische Untersuchung und Einführung* (Münster i. W.: Aschendorff, 1931).

——. *Die Geschichte der Katholischen Theologie seit dem Ausgang der Vaterzeit* (Freiburg i. Br.: Herder, 1933).

——. *Die Kulturphilosophie des hl. Thomas von Aquin* (Augsburg, 1925).

——. *Mittelalterliches Geistesleben* (Munich: Heuber, 1926).

——. *Einführung in der Summa Theologiae* (Freiburg i. Br., 1919).

Gregorian University. *De operibus S. Roberti Bellarmini* (Rome, 1930).

Guelluy, Robert. *Philosophie et théologie chez Guillaume d'Ockham* (Louvain, 1947).

Hamman, G. A. *La doctrine de l'église et de l'état chez Occam: étude sur le Breviloquium* (aux éditions franciscaines, Paris, 1942).

Harris, C. R. S. *Duns Scotus* (London: Clarendon Press, 1927).

Heredia, Beltran de. *La herencia literaria del Maestro Fray Francisco de Victoria: los manuscriptos des Maestro Victoria* (Valencia: Biblioteca de Tomistae Españoles, 1928).

Ibranyi, Francis. *Ethica secundum S. Thomam et Kant* (Rome: Angelico, 1931).

Karl, W. *Die Lehre vom Primat des Willens bei Augustinus, Duns Scotus, und Descartes* (Strassburg, 1886).

Kaxenberger, P. K. *Assertiones centum ad mentem subtilis ac Mariani Joannis Duns Scoti* (editio nova, Quaracchi, 1906).

Lagarde, Georges de. *La naissance de l'esprit laique au déclin du moyen âge* (Paris: Presses Universitaires de France, 1948).

Landry, Bernard. *Duns Scot* (Paris: Alcan, 1922).

Lauer, H. *Die Moraltheologie Alberts des Grossen* (Freiburg i. Br.: Herder, 1911).

Leclercq, J. *Leçons de droit naturel* (Paris, 1929).

Ledesma, Martin. *Commentaria in IV libros Sententiarum* (Coimbre, 1555–60).

Ledesma, Pierre. *In I partem Summae Theologicae* (Salamanca, 1596, 1611).

Lehu, Leonard, O.P. *La raison règle de la moralité d'après Saint Thomas* (Paris: Gabalda, 1930).

Le Senne, René. *Traité de morale générale* (Paris: Presses Universitaires de France, 1949).

Longpré, P. E. *La philosophie du B. Duns Scot* (Paris, 1924).

Lottin, Odon, O.S.B. *Le droit naturel chez S. Thomas et ses prédécesseurs* (Bruges: Beyaert, 1931).

————. *Principes de morale* (Louvain: Mt. César, 1947).

————. *Psychologie et morale aux XII e et XIII e siècles* (Louvain: Mt. César, [t. I] 1942, [t. II] 1948, [t. III] 1949).

Lutz, Eduard. *Die Psychologie Bonaventuras* (Münster i. W.: Aschendorff, 1909).

Mahieu, Leon. *François Suarez, sa philosophie et les rapports qu'elle a avec sa théologie* (Paris: Desclée, 1921).

Mandonnet, Pierre, O.P. *Mélanges Mandonnet* (Paris: Vrin, 1930).

Maritain, Jacques. *Science and Wisdom,* translated by Bernard Wall (London: G. Bles, The Centenary Press, 1940).

————. *The Rights of Man and Natural Law,* translated by Doris C. Anson (New York: Charles Scribner's Sons, 1943).

————. *The Degrees of Knowledge* (New York: Charles Scribner's Sons, 1938).

————. *Person et Individu* (Rome: Marietti, 1946).

————. *Éléments de philosophie* (Paris: Tequi, 1922).

————. *Primauté du spirituel* (Paris: Plon, 1927).

Mausbach, Joseph. *Die Ethik des Heiligen Augustinus* (Freiburg i. Br.: Herder, 1929).

———. *Grundlage und Ausbildung des Character nach dem hl. Thomas von Aquin* (Freiburg, 1911).

Meersseman, G. M., O.P. *Introductio in opera omnia B. Alberti Magni,* apud C. Beyaert (Bruges, 1931).

Minges, P. P., O.F.M. *Ioannis Duns Scoti, doctrina philosophica et theologica quoad res praecipuas proposita et exposita* (Quaracchi, 1930).

———. *Ist Duns Skotus Indeterminist?* (Münster i. W.: Aschendorff, 1905).

———. *Der Gottesbegriff des Duns Scotus auf seinen angeblich excessiven Indeterminismus geprüft* (Wien, 1906).

Miscellanea Moralia. In Honorem Eximii Domini Arthur Janssen (Louvain: Nauwelaerts, 1948).

Montefortino, H. de. *Venerabilis Johannis Duns Scoti Summa Theologica ex universis operibus eius concinnata* (Rome, 1900).

Müller, Wilhelm. *Der Statt in seinen Beziehungen zur sittlichen Ordnung bei Thomas von Aquin* (Münster i. W.: Aschendorff, 1916).

Muller-Thym, B. J. *The Establishment of the University of Being in the Doctrine of Meister Eckhart of Hochheim* (New York: Sheed and Ward, 1939).

Paulus, Jean. *Henri de Gand: Essai sur les tendances de sa metaphysique* (Paris: Vrin, 1938).

Peghaire, J., C.S.Sp. *Intellectus et ratio selon S. Thomas d'Aquin* (Ottawa: Institut d'études médiévales, 1936).

Pegis, Anton C. *St. Thomas and the Problem of the Soul in the Thirteenth Century* (Toronto: Medieval Studies, 1934).

————. *St. Thomas and the Greeks* (Milwaukee: Marquette Univ. Press, 1939).

Pelster, F., S.J. *Kritische Studien zum Leben und zu den Schriften Alberts des Grossen* (Freiburg, 1920).

Pieper, J. *Die ontische Grundlage des Sittlichen nach Thomas von Aquin* (Münster i. W.: Helios, 1929).

Quetif, J., and Echard, J., O.P. *Scriptores ordinis praedicatorum* (Paris, 1719, 1721).

Rager, John C. *Political Philosophy of Blessed Cardinal Bellarmine* (Washington, D.C.: Catholic Univ. of Amer., 1926).

Reilly, George C. *The Psychology of St. Albert the Great Compared with that of St. Thomas* (Washington, D.C.: Catholic Univ. of Amer., 1934).

Renard, G. *Le droit, la justice et la volonté* (Paris: Tenin, 1924).

————. *Le droit, la logique et le bon sens* (Paris: Tenin, 1925).

————. *Le droit, l'ordre et la raison* (Paris: Tenin, 1927).

————. *La valeur de la loi* (Paris: Sirey, 1928).

————. *La théorie de l'institution,* Vol. I, partie juridique (Paris: Sirey, 1930).

Rietter, Anton. *Die Moral des heiligen Thomas von Aquin* (München: Lentner'schen, 1858).

Rohmer, Jean. *La finalité morale chez les théologiens de Saint Augustin à Duns Scot* (Paris: Vrin, 1939).

Roland-Gosselin, Bernard. *La doctrine politique de Saint Thomas d'Aquin* (Paris: Rivière, 1928).

———. *La morale de Saint Augustin* (Paris: Rivière, 1925).

Rousselot, P. *Pour l'histoire du problème de l'amour au moyen âge* (Münster i. W.: Aschendorff, 1908).

———. *The Intellectualism of Saint Thomas* (London: Sheed and Ward, 1935).

Ryan, E., S.J. *The Historical Scholarship of St. Bellarmine* (New York: Fordham University Press, 1936).

Saint-Maurice, Beraud de. *Jean Duns Scot, un docteur des temps nouveaux* (Montreal: Therien frères limitée, 1944).

Scorraille, Raoul de, S.J. *François Suarez de la Compagnie de Jesus* (Paris: Lethielleux, 1912).

Scott, James B. *The Catholic Conception of International Law* (Washington, D.C.: Georgetown Univ. Press, 1934).

———. *The Spanish Origin of International Law: lectures on Francisco de Vitoria and Francisco Suarez* (Washington, D.C.: The School of Foreign Service, Georgetown University, 1928).

Seiler, Julius. *Der Zweck in der Philosophie des Franz Suarez* (Innsbruck, 1936).

Sertillanges, A.-D. *La philosophie morale de S. Thomas d'Aquin* (2nd ed., Paris: Alcan, 1946).

———. *Saint Thomas d'Aquin* (Paris: Alcan, 1925).

———. *Les grandes thèses de la philosophie thomiste* (Paris: Bloud, 1928).

————. *La philosophie des lois* (Paris: Alsatia, 1946).

Serviere, R. P. de la. *La théologie de Bellarmin* (Paris, 1908).

Six, K., Grabmann, Hatheyer, Inanen, and Biederlack. *Beiträge zur Philosophie des P. Suarez* (Innsbruck, 1917).

————. *P. F. Suarez, Gedankenblätter zu seinem dreihundertjahrigen Todestage* (Innsbruck, 1917).

Stang. *La notion de loi dans S. Thomas d'Aquin* (Paris: Bossuet, 1927).

Switalski, Bruno, C.SS.R. *Neoplatonism and the Ethics of St. Augustine* (New York: Polish Institute of Arts and Sciences in America, 1946).

Taparelli d'Azeglio. *Essai théorique de droit naturel basé sur les faits* (Paris: Tournai, 1875).

Ternus, J., S.J. *Zur Vorgeschichte der Moralsysteme von Vitoria bis Medina* (Paderborn, 1931).

Thils, G. *Tendances actuelles en théologie morale* (Mechliniae: Gembloux, Duculot, 1940).

Tornay, S. C. *Ockham: Studies and Selections* (La Salle, Ill.: The Open Court Publishing Co., 1938).

Touron, A. *Histoire des hommes illustres de l'ordre de Saint Dominique*, Vol. IV (Paris, 1743).

Ullman, Walter. *The Medieval Idea of Law* (London: Methuen, 1946).

Vacant, A. *La philosophie de Duns Scot comparée à celle de St. Thomas* (Paris, 1889).

Van Hove, A. *De legibus ecclesiasticis* (Malines, 1930).

Vermeersch-Creusen. *Epitome Iuris Canonici* (Rome: Dessain, 1933).

Vignaux, Paul. *Justification et prédestination au XIV* *siècle* (Paris: Leroux, 1934).

———. *Luther, commentateur des Sentences* (Paris: Vrin, 1935).

Vilmain, J. *Die Staatslehre des Thomas von Aquin im Lichte mod. polit. Jurist.* (Leipzig, 1910).

Vlissingen, C. a, O.F.M.Cap. *De evolutione definitionis iuris gentium* (Rome: Gregorian University, 1940).

Wadding, Luke. *Annales minorum seu trium ordinum a S. Francisco institutorum,* prope Florentiam (Quaracchi, 1931).

———. *Scriptores ordinis minorum* (Rome, 1650).

Waffelaert. *Étude de théologie morale sur l'obligation en conscience des lois civiles* (Tournai, 1884).

Werner, Karl. *Die Scholastik des späteren Mittelalters* (Wien: Braumüller, 1881–87).

———. *F. Suarez und die Scholastik der letzten Jahrhunderte* (2nd ed., Ratisbonne, 1889).

Wilms, H., O.P. *Albert the Great* (London: Burns Oates and Washbourne, Ltd., 1933).

Wittmann, Michael. *Die Ethik des hl. Thomas von Aquin* (München: Heuber, 1933).

Wulf, M. de. *Études sur Henri de Gand* (Paris, 1897).

Zuidema, Sytse Ulbe. *De Philosophie Van Occam in Zijn Commentaar Op De Sententien* (Hilversum: Schipper, 1936).

Articles

Adler, M. J. "A Question about Law," *Essays in Thomism* (New York: Sheed and Ward, 1942), pp. 205–36.

Baudry, Leon. "La prescience divine chez Saint Anselme," *Archives d'histoire doctrinale et littéraire du moyen âge,* XIII, 223–38.

Blic, J. de. "Le volontarisme juridique chez Suarez," *Revue de philosophie,* New Series, X (Jan.-Dec., 1930), 213–30.

Bourgeois, R. "La théorie de la connaissance intellectuelle chez Henri de Gand," *Revue de philosophie,* XXXVI (1936), 238–59.

Bourke, Vernon J. "The Provenance of the De Apprehensione," *Speculum,* XVII (Jan., 1943), 91–98.

Brochard, V. "La morale ancienne et la morale moderne," *Revue philosophique* (Jan., 1901), pp. 7 ff.

Brouillard, R. "Suarez," *Dictionnaire de théologie catholique,* XIV (1941), 2638–2728.

Chroust, Anton-Hermann. "Philosophy of Law from St. Augustine to St. Thomas Aquinas," *New Scholasticism,* XX (Jan., 1946), 26–71.

D'Alencon, P. Edouard. "Castro," *Dictionnaire de théologie catholique,* II (1932), 1835 f.

Doncoeur, P. "Le nominalisme de Guillaume Occam, théorie de la relation," *Revue néo-scholastique,* XXIII (1921), 5–25.

Drouin, F. M., O.P. "Le libre arbitre selon Albert le Grand," *Publications de l'institut d'études médiévales d'Ottawa,* I–II (1932), 91–120.

Elter, E., S.J. "Norma honestatis ad mentem Divi Thomae," *Gregorianum,* VIII (1927), 337–57.

Eschmann, I. T., O.P. "A Thomistic Glossary on the Preeminence of a Common Good," *Medieval Studies,* V (Toronto, 1943), 123–65.

Feckes, K. "Die Rechtfertigungslehre des Gabriel Biel und ihre Stellung innerhalb der nominalistichen Schule," *Theologische Quartalschrift* (Münster, 1925), pp. 50–76.

Garrigou-Lagrange, R. "Du charactère metaphysique de la théologie morale de Saint Thomas," *Revue Thomiste* (1925), pp. 341–55.

————. "La prudence: sa place dans l'organisme des virtus," *Revue Thomiste,* IX (1926), 411–16.

Gillet, M. S., O.P. "Conscience chrétienne et justice sociale," *Ed. de la revue des jeunes,* Vol. XVI (Paris, 1922).

————. "Le moral et la social d'après S. Thomas," *Mélanges thomistes* (1923), pp. 311–26.

————. "Les jugements de valeur à la conception positive de la morale," *Revue des sciences philosophique et théologique,* Vol. VI, Part 2 (1912), pp. 5–31.

Gilson, Étienne. "L'Âme raisonnable chez Albert le Grand," *Archives d'histoire doctrinale et littérairé du moyen âge,* XIV, 5–72.

Gonzales, M.-C., O.P. "De imperfectione morali," *Études et recherches, théologie,* Cahiers II–III (Ottawa, 1944), pp. 227–374.

Gorce, M. M. "Medina," *Dictionnaire de théologie catholique,* X (1928), 482–85.

Grabmann, Martin. "Der Einfluss Alberts des Grossen auf das mittelalterliche Geistesleben," *Zeitschrift für Katholische Theologie,* LII (1928), 153–82; 313–56.

Harmignie, P. "Ordonnances humaines et obligation de conscience," *Revue néo-scholastique de philosophie,* XXXII (1930), 267–320.

Heredia, Beltran de. "El maestro Domingo (Francisco) de Soto," *La Ciencia Tomista,* XLIII (1931), 357–73.

———. "Soto," *Dictionnaire de théologie catholique,* XIV (1941), 2423–31.

Jansen, Bernhard, S.J. "Die scholastische Philosophie des 17. Jahrhunderts," *Philosophisches Jahrbuch,* Band L (1937), pp. 401–44.

———. "Die Pflege der Philosophie im Jesuitenorden während des 17./18. Jahrhunderts," *Philosophisches Jahrbuch* (1938), Heft 3, pp. 344–66; Heft 4, pp. 435–56.

Janssens, E. "La coutume, source formelle de droit, d'après S. Thomas d'Aquin et d'après Suarez," *Revue Thomiste,* New Series, XIV (July 1931), 681–726.

Jombart, E., S.J. "La coutume d'après Suarez et le code de droit canonique," *Nouvelle revue théologique,* LIX (1932), 769–84.

———. "La volontarisme de la loi d'après Suarez," *Nouvelle revue théologique,* LIX (1932), 34–44.

Lagarde, Georges de. "La philosophie sociale d'Henri de Gand et Godefroid de Fontaines," *Archives d'histoire doctrinale et littéraire du moyen âge,* XVIII (1943), 73–142.

Lajard, F. "Henri de Gand," *Histoire de la France,* XX (1842), 144–203.

La Porte, Jean. "Le libre arbitre et l'attention selon Saint Thomas," *Revue de metaphysique et de la morale* (1931), pp. 61 ff.; (1932), pp. 201 ff.; (1934), pp. 25 ff.

Le Bachelet, X. "Bellarmine," *Dictionnaire de théologie catholique,* II (1932), 560–99.

Ledrus, M., S.J. "Le probleme des lois purement penales," *Nouvelle revue théologique,* LIX (1932), 45–56.

Lehu, Leonard, O.P. "À quel point précis de la Somme Theol. commence le traité de la moralité," *Revue Thomiste,* XXXIII (1928), 521–32.

———. "À propos de la règle de la moralité," *Revue des sciences philosophiques et théologiques,* XVII (1929), 449–66.

Lottin, Odon, O.S.B. "La definition classique de la loi," *Revue néo-scholastique de philosophie* (1925), pp. 129–45; 244–73.

———. "Les eléments de la moralité des actes chez St. Thomas d'Aquin," *Revue néo-scholastique de philosophie,* XXIV (1922), pp. 281 ff. XXV (1923), pp. 56 ff.

———. "Albert et l'ethique à Nicomaque," *Beiträge zur Geschichte der Philosophie des Mittelalters,* Supplement. III, Halbband 1 (1935), pp. 611–26.

———. "Les premiers linéaments du traité de la syndérèse au moyen âge," *Revue néo-scholastique de philosophie,* XXVIII (1926), 422–54.

————. "Traité du Chancelier Philippe sur la syndérèse," *Revue néo-scholastique de philosophie,* XXIX (1927), 208–23.

————. "Le créateur du traité de la syndérèse," *Revue néo-scholastique de philosophie,* XXIX (1927), 197–208.

————. "La syndérèse chez Albert le Grand et Saint Thomas d'Aquin," *Revue néo-scholastique de philosophie,* XXX (1928), 18–44.

————. "Le problème de la moralité intrinsèque d'Abelard à Saint Thomas," *Revue Thomiste,* New Series, XVIII (1934), 477–515.

————. "L'Ordre morale et l'ordre logique d'après Saint Thomas d'Aquin," *Annales de l'institut superieur de philosophie,* V (1924), 303–99.

Mandonnet, Pierre, O.P. "Bañez," *Dictionnaire de théologie catholique,* II (1932), 139–45.

Maritain, Jacques. "Action: The Perfection of Human Life," *Sewanee Review,* Vol. LVI (1948), no. 1, pp. 1–11.

Martyniak, C. "La définition thomiste de la loi," *Revue de philosophie,* XXXVII (Jan.-Dec., 1930), 231–50.

Mausbach, J. "Zur Begriffsbestimmung des sittlich Guten," *Philosophisches Jahrbuch der Görresgesellschaft,* Band X (1899), Heft 4, pp. 303–18; 407–21.

Merkelbach, B., O.P. "Le traité des actions humaines dans la morale thomiste," *Revue des sciences philosophique et théologique,* XV (1926), 185–207.

Minges, P. P., O.F.M. "Der angebliche excessive realismus des Duns Scotus," *Beiträge zur Geschichte der Philosophie des Mittelalters,* Band VII (1908), Heft 1, pp. 1–108.

Muñoz, Jesus, S.J. "Escencia del Libre Albedrio y Proceso del Acto Libre según F. Romeo, O.P., Sto. Tomás y F. Suarez, S.J.," *Miscelanea Comillas,* IX (Universidad Pontifica Comillas, 1948), 349–504.

Murray, J. C., S.J. "St. Robert Bellarmine on the Indirect Power," *Theological Studies* (Dec., 1948), pp. 491–535.

O'Sullivan, R. "Medieval Idea of Law," *The Month,* CLXXXIII (Jan., 1947), 35–39.

Peghaire, J., C.S.Sp. "La causalité du bien selon Albert le Grand," *Études d'histoire littéraire et doctrinale du XIII e siècle,* II (1932), 59–89.

Pegis, Anton C. "Matter, Beatitude and Liberty," Maritain Volume of *The Thomist,* V (Jan., 1943), 265–80.

Pelster, Franz. "Eine Kontroverse über die Methode der Moraltheologie aus dem Ende des 16. Jahrhunderts. Michael Bartholmaeus Salon, O.E.S.A. und Dominikus Banez, O.P.," *Scholastik,* XVII (1942), 385–411.

Radonic, B. "La loi d'après Duns Scot," *Nova Revija,* XVII (1939), 133–43.

Revue Thomiste: Special Number—Cajetan, XXXIX (1934–35), 1–503.

Rohner, M., O.P. "Kommentor des hl. Albertus Magnus zur Einführung in die Politik des Aristotles," *Divus Thomas* (Freiburg, 1932), pp. 95 ff.

Roland-Gosselin, M.-D., O.P. "Sur le double rédaction par Albert le Grand de sa dispute contre Averroes,"

Archives d'histoire doctrinale et littéraire du moyen âge, I, 309–12.

Ruch, C. "Biel," *Dictionnaire de théologie catholique*, II (1932), 814–25.

Schneider, Arthur C. "Die Psychologie Alberts des Grossen," *Beiträge zur Geschichte der Philosophie des Mittelalters*, Band IV (1903), Heft. 5–6, pp. 1–548.

Schubert, P. A., S.V.D. "Augustins Lex-Aeterna-Lehre nach Inhalt und Quellen," *Beiträge zur Geschichte der Philosophie des Mittelalters*, Band XXIV (1924), Heft 2, pp. 1–63.

Sertillanges, A.-D. "L'Activité morale d'après S. Thomas d'Aquin," *Revue Thomiste*, XXXIII (1928), 497–520.

———. "La morale ancienne et la morale moderne," *Revue philosophique de la France et de l'étranger* (Jan.-June, 1901), pp. 280–92.

Sheets, J. R., S.J. "Justice in the Moral Thought of St. Anselm," *The Modern Schoolman*, XXV (Jan., 1948), 132–39.

Simonin, H. D. "Autour de la solution thomiste du problème de l'amour," *Archives d'histoire doctrinale et littéraire du moyen âge* (1931), pp. 174–274.

Stöckerl, D. "Castro," *Lexikon für Theologie und Kirche*, I (1930), 261.

Tonneau, P., O.P. "Imperfection," *Bulletin Thomiste* (1930–33), pp. 783 ff.

Toso, A. "De conceptu legis iuxta Aquinatis doctrinam," *Jus Pontificium: seu Ephemerides*, IV (1924), 31–36.

Ulpianas, Lopes, S.J. "Theoria legis mere poenalis et hodiernae leges civiles," *Periodica*, XXVII (1938), pp. 203 ff.

Vangheluwe, V. "De lege mere poenali," *Ephemerides theologiae Lovanienses* (Apr.-Jul., 1939), pp. 383–429.

————. "De ortu atque profectu sententiae disiunctivae in explicanda lege pure poenali," *Miscellanea moralia* (Louvain: Nauwelaerts, 1948), pp. 209–24.

Van Hove, A. "Quelques publications récentes au sujet des lois purement pénales," *Miscellanea moralia* (Louvain: Nauwelaerts, 1948), pp. 225–53.

Walz, A. "De genuino titulo Summae Theologiae," *Angelicum*, XVIII (1941), 142–51.

Wittmann, Michael. "Thomas von Aquin und Bonaventura in ihrer Glückseligkeitslehre," *Beiträge zur Geschichte der Philosophie des Mittelalters*, Supplement. III (1935), pp. 749–58.

IMPRIMI POTEST

Daniel H. Conway, S.J.
Provincial
Missouri Province
St. Louis, Mo., Sept. 22, 1950

NIHIL OBSTAT

Innocentius Swoboda, O.F.M.
Censor Librorum

IMPRIMATUR

✠ Joseph Ritter
Archiepiscopus
Sti. Ludovici, die 6 Augusti, 1951

INDEX